MAKING VIRTUAL WORLDS

MAKING VIRTUAL WORLDS

LINDEN LAB AND SECOND LIFE

THOMAS M. MALABY

CORNELL UNIVERSITY PRESS
ITHACA AND LONDON

First published 2009 by Cornell University Press

Printed in the United States of America

Book design by Scott Levine

Library of Congress Cataloging-in-Publication Data

Malaby, Thomas M., 1967–
    Making virtual worlds : Linden Lab and Second Life / Thomas M. Malaby.
        p. cm.
    Includes bibliographical references and index.
    ISBN 978-0-8014-4746-4 (cloth : alk. paper)
    1. Second Life (Game)—Social aspects.   2. Linden Lab (Firm).   3. Shared virtual environments—Case studies.   4. Computer games—Design—Social aspects—Case studies.   5. Business anthropology—California—San Francisco—Case studies.   6. Corporate culture—California—San Francisco—Case studies.   I. Title.
    GV1469.25.S425M35 2009
    794.8—dc22   2008052550

FOR SAMUEL AND JULIAN

CONTENTS

ACKNOWLEDGMENTS

In the course of this project I have relied on the good graces, brilliance, and support of many people. First, I want to express my appreciation to Linden Lab, for being willing to let an anthropologist cross into their domain of synthesis and world creation. In an industry only just now learning what it can learn from researchers, Linden Lab has been a pioneer. Philip Rosedale, Robin Harper, and Cory Ondrejka deserve special thanks for being open to the continued presence of the anthropologist who dropped into their midst. To the many Lindens who sacrificed their precious coffee time to help me understand how they worked and saw the world, I extend my deepest appreciation and thanks.

The research upon which this work is based was conducted with the vital support of the National Science Foundation, through its subprogram on Ethics and Values Studies in the Science and Society Program (grant #0423043), and by a fellowship from the Center for 21st Century Studies at the University of Wisconsin–Milwaukee. A fellowship at the University of Wisconsin–Madison's Institute for Research in the Humanities provided support during the writing of the book, and the community of scholars there were a regular source of stimulating conversation for the project.

Portions of chapter 1, before extensive modifications, appeared in two articles of mine: Malaby 2006a and Malaby 2007b. I thank the publishers of those original articles for allowing me to extend and develop those texts and my ideas here.

I am deeply indebted to many colleagues and friends for their willingness to comment on this work in its prepublication form, including Julian Dibbell, Tim Burke, Gabriella Coleman, Alex Golub, Dan Hunter, F. Gregory Lastowka, Ren Reynolds, Kalman Applbaum, Ingrid Jordt, Paul Brodwin, Sandra Braman, Gordon Calleja, Bonnie Nardi, and Douglas Thomas. The community at the blog Terra Nova was also an invaluable source of thoughtful commentary on several early forays into this material. James Paul Gee, Kurt Squire, Constance Steinkuehler, and the graduate students of the Games, Learning, and Society Program at the University of Wisconsin–Madison were incredibly welcoming and gave important feedback following several presentations there of many of these ideas.

Peter Wissoker at Cornell University Press helped shepherd this book from its beginnings as a set of ideas to a manuscript; our extended chats about the book were critical to its rounding into form. Carolyn Pouncy whipped the text into shape with a steady hand, and Susan Specter deftly oversaw the transformation of text into tome. Many thanks to them all.

Throughout this project, I relied heavily on two exceptional havens from research and writing. The first was my adopted home in California during my research, and I will surely never repay the debt of hospitality that Andrew Guzman and Jeannie Sears extended to me time and time again. The second was, and is, my adopted home online, the community of researchers in World of Warcraft that has been a place where everyone knows not only my toon name but also their social theory.

Finally, I am ever grateful for the patience and understanding of my partner in all things, Cristina Hernandez-Malaby, as well as the sustaining presence of Julian and Samuel, gamers all.

INTRODUCTION: A DEVELOPER'S-EYE VIEW

I am standing in front of a whiteboard—the dry-erase boards seemingly ubiquitous in high tech company offices—looking at a drawing that offers a bird's-eye view of Santorini on a letter-sized color printout taped to the board. At least I think this is Santorini, a picturesque Greek island formed from the remnants of a collapsed volcano. In the picture I can see its c-shaped landmass, its steeply rising elevation, indicated by a panoply of colors, all surrounded by a deep blue that also fills its bay, where a smaller island sits. A Cartesian grid divides up the image into neat squares, more than four hundred in all. I had done my first ethnographic field research in Greece, ten years prior, though I had never made it to Santorini (ethnographers feel a keen imperative to spend every possible moment at their "field site"; in my case that was Chania, Crete). Now it is February 2005, and I am in a dimly lit yet loftlike space in San Francisco, at the offices of Linden Lab, makers of the virtual world Second Life. The image, with its god's eye perspective and posted in this work setting, suggests strongly the practice of design, even creation in the large sense. This is a piece of a world that is also an object of work. But at the time my perspective gravitated toward the experiential: I was thinking that soon I will be able to walk—and fly—around at least this homage to Santorini. Within a month, I had done so.

Virtual worlds require less of an introduction by the day, as they have risen dramatically to prominence in a number of quarters.[1] They are characterized by their use of Internet connectivity to provide a persistent, open-ended, and shared three-dimensional space in which users can interact, typically via avatars (virtual bodies that move about and act inside the world). Second Life, launched in June 2003, stands in contrast to many of the other well-known virtual worlds (World of Warcraft, Everquest II, Lineage II) in that it has no established and universal game objectives. Users spend their time in Second Life doing numerous different kinds of things. Many of them socialize via text-based chat (more recently, voice capability has been added), and while they do this they may also be dancing through their avatars or playing games or just enjoying a nice view. Second Life has thus quickly risen to prominence as the most celebrated "social" virtual world. Beyond its remarkable growth (at the time of this writing, February 2008, it has millions of registered users and by some accounts about 600,000 active users), its distinctive feature is its users' access to in-world "tools" for the creation of interactive virtual objects and other content to which they own the intellectual property rights.[2] Users can, furthermore, control how these creations are distributed to other users, including through market transactions in the in-world currency, Linden dollars (L$).

The land (like that shown on the image I pondered) is also a purchasable commodity in Second Life, and this combination seems to have contributed to the emergence of a remarkable economy, one that also supports buying and selling Linden dollars for U.S. dollars. In short, Second Life supports the production of various forms of capital (social, cultural and market), and this in turn has provided a framework for continuing innovations in Second Life's use by individual and institutional participants, many of whom have begun not only to pursue market interests but also to explore the potential of Second Life for learning and therapy. The environment now provides a home for a wide range of nonvirtual institutions, from Harvard Law School and

Reuters News Service, to U.S. presidential campaign offices, therapeutic communities, and financial establishments.

When I began doing research at Linden Lab in December 2004, approximately thirteen thousand users had created accounts in Second Life—small by the standards of the virtual world industry (at the time the original Lineage, a game primarily popular in East Asia, boasted over two million users worldwide), but this number was beginning to rise at an increasing rate, and this lent a sense of urgency and hope to the employees of Linden Lab over that year. I visited the company every month between December 2004 and January 2006, for one to three weeks at a time (usually during business hours, but including after hours get-togethers as well), and while local I focused on face-to-face participant observation along with interviews. I conducted twelve lengthy, recorded, semi-structured interviews (one to two hours, on average) with employees from all over the company, including management, and conducted over forty-five informal, unrecorded interviews (fifteen to forty-five minutes, on average) with Lindens (employees of Linden Lab, as they call themselves) over coffee or during breaks from their work.[3] These were supplemented by innumerable brief exchanges and other interactions. I also did some light work for Linden Lab (nothing that put me in contact with Second Life users) in order better to understand their work practice, including the use of in-world tools. To the extent that the company was small (thirty-five employees at the start, sixty-seven at the conclusion) and for the most part all working in the same building (even the same room), this continued to be effective.[4] I benefited greatly from Linden Lab's open office environment, with employees each occupying desks grouped in clusters in a large room.

Early on I realized that Lindens were incorporating a wide array of communications media into their work practice (as, of course, many people do these days). The workers demonstrated a familiarity and ease with "in-world" affordances (that is, communication tools available inside Second Life), which they seamlessly included in how they went about their jobs. As it became clear that some of their work was itself virtual—themselves making "work" use of the very world they provided for their users—I began to do research in Second Life as well. This allowed me to continue to use my time when not in San Francisco to conduct research. While I rely most heavily on the face-to-face research in what follows, I also at times refer to in-world experiences, e-mail and instant messaging exchanges, Web-based resources, and other media.[5] It also bears mentioning that this is a work that attempts to capture things as Lindens saw them with regard to themselves and Second Life in 2005, not an account of how the users of Second Life saw many of the same events—the limitations and possibilities of speaking about a shared culture among Second Life users has been extensively treated by Tom Boellstorff (2008).

This book does not offer a comprehensive account of the practices, meanings, and history of Linden Lab as a conventional ethnography might. While certainly the small number of its employees would make such a thorough treatment ethically troublesome, the broader reason is because this book has a different aim. Following the path set by Paul Rabinow's *Making PCR: A Study in Biotechnology* (1996), to which the title of this book is a respectful homage, this work illuminates ethnographically complex processes of governance, games, and creativity. These processes are so much a part of the rise not only of virtual worlds but of multiple settings in which our technologized experience is both open-ended and architected. The book also asks why virtual worlds matter and which factors cause things to be at stake within them. These primary issues determine the structure of the book, with alternating chapters addressing the larger questions regarding virtual worlds and the ways that the employees of Linden Lab wrestled with the questions of how to manage in what they hoped would be a nonhierarchical fashion. Anyone seeking to understand the impact of the digital on new forms of institutions and their relationship to individual creativity needs to ask the questions I raise here. Linden Lab in 2005 is, I argue, a particularly revealing case for developing that understanding through an ethnographic treatment.

By the time I finished my research in January 2006, more than 120,000 user accounts had been created, and Second Life was beginning to appear with greater and greater frequency in national and international news outlets. This tenfold increase in 2005 points to the importance of this year in the broader history of Second Life and Linden Lab. The Lindens could not know that a future of more than six hundred thousand active users awaited them. Instead, 2005 was the year in which Second Life moved from obscurity to being buzz-worthy. The optimism this fostered around Linden Lab was nonetheless guarded, for while many companies might count such growth as a proof of the rightness of their strategy and direction, Linden Lab's work practice and discourse were instead marked by a constant awareness of their own lack of control over what Second Life was and could become, and how every move they made was in many respects a shot in the dark. The new landmass I stood pondering was a good example of just this kind of gambit.

The "atoll," as it was referred to around Linden Lab that winter and spring, was part of an ambitious plan begun in late 2004 and continuing through early 2005.[6] As the demand for land grew with the population of Second Life, the content team (the Linden employees in charge of providing the land and other basic infrastructure of Second Life) was scrambling to get ahead of the curve. Needing to be ready to bring online a lot of new land as growth increased, but wanting to do more than just attach more ground to the "mainland" continent already in existence (which was beginning to look more and more amorphous), the members of the team decided to design an entirely new continent to the north of the old one, which they would bring online in pieces as needed. (The size of "continents" in Second Life is not really comparable to continents offline—they are much smaller relative to human/avatar size; although the atoll's size relative to the real Santorini may be similar, the atoll looms much larger in Second Life, especially in comparison to Second Life's "islands," which range from 1/400th to 1/100th of the atoll's size.) The team members sought to bring an interesting and aesthetically "coherent" shape to Second Life on a grand scale, one with a dramatic topography and correspondingly scenic vistas. But they decided to go further and build structures and other objects on this atoll that would themselves, they hoped, be meaningful.

This content would be archeological—the remains of an imagined past civilization that had moved slowly up the atoll in altitude as it advanced technologically (and then departed for "space," almost as the first Second Life explorer—a Linden-created user named Magellan Linden—arrived). This contrived civilization had an iconography, built around the totemlike presence of the moth, which the content team found amusing and inspirational at the same time—a constant moving upward toward the light (the sun—Second Life had four-hour day/night cycles, complete with a sun and a moon) defined its "prehistory" on the island. It had distinct building styles, such as the corrugated steel and whitewashed colors of some structures built on platforms over the water of the bay, and it incorporated more advanced technology in new, higher areas. This strategy of making not only a landmass but also a civilization with a "mythology" to accompany it was a response to something the content team (and other Lindens, though there was not a uniform consensus about this) saw as a "problem" with user creation on the mainland: it was "ugly" or "trashy." Half-finished castles stood next to huge egg-shaped buildings next to giant flashing, rotating advertisements next to log cabins. The team's hope with the atoll project was to prompt residents to explore and expand on a design style together and thus realize one of the values that hung like a promise over Second Life (and Linden Lab, as we shall see): enlightened creativity, with an attendant aesthetic payoff. More broadly, such a combination of top-down contrivance and (hoped-for) bottom-up emergence was emblematic of Linden Lab's approach to governing Second Life (and itself).

The atoll was brought online piece by piece—each square in the grid that overlaid it represented one "simulator" or "sim," itself powered by one server (the size of each sim, relative to avatar size, is sixteen "acres" in-world). The content team watched with interest to see what the residents would do, and indeed in some places residents built with an eye toward the content already in place. With some users employing the matching textures (image files that could be "wrapped" around objects to give them a "texture") and other things Linden Lab provided for free at in-world "kiosks" (effectively, virtual vending machines), neighborhoods with a consistency of style emerged here and there. But on the whole the engagement of the "mythology" of the past civilization was not extensive, and in many cases, especially commercial buildings, there were no common stylistic elements at all. By early 2006 the island was dominated by the same heterogeneous mix of stuff as the old continent.

By that time Linden Lab's content team appeared disillusioned with the prospect of prompting aesthetically compelling, collaborative content within Second Life on a large scale. At the same time, however, a related development did lead to some thematic coherence—if not, from the content team's point of view, high aesthetic value. This was the result of a significant shift in residents' relationship to land itself following an update to the Second Life software (version 1.6). More and more private islands were being sold (at approximately US$1,000 apiece) and these owners—typically powerful residents with lots of real-estate holdings—were "renting" space to other residents. Making use of the greater sovereignty islands afforded them (as compared to the mainland), they built neighborhoods of a particular style, much like offline suburban developments in the United States. These island owners made spaces that appealed to consumers who wanted a place to live in Second Life, ready-made and with clear zoning restrictions (contained in every renter's agreement with the island owner, much like a covenant in real estate). The lesson contained in this unintended consequence was for Lindens a familiar one: their efforts to prompt user behavior of one sort or another were fraught with complexities, as a number of ongoing processes collided with their own interventions. As one developer said about another initiative of Linden Lab that did not take off as expected (this one making it possible for users to stream video from their own personal computer into Second Life): "There's something that we're missing here. There's some piece that will totally change its usability, and I don't know what that is."

This reveals something distinctive about Second Life as a product. Of course, all companies proceed knowing that the market may surprise them, and this has become an important thread in our understanding of marketing and consumption. As Timothy Burke (1996), for example, has explored at length, for Colgate and other companies seeking to market hygiene products in Zimbabwe unexpected uses (such as toothpaste for ringworm) posed a challenge of marketing. Which emergent practices should be further marketed (that is, supported)? Which should be ignored or dissuaded? But for conventional products such as these, the product's use is nonetheless dictated principally by the manufacturer, and in a relatively narrow fashion. Colgate was not banking on its customers continually finding new uses for toothpaste.

Second Life is not this kind of product. Like few other products we can identify—early telephone service is one, Internet search engines may be another—Second Life *depends* on unanticipated uses by its consumers. Value in Second Life is highly dependent on a contrived architecture, and it thereby radically reconfigures how human effort accumulates in various forms of capital. In a very important sense Second Life, with so much of its content created by users themselves, was meant to make itself, and this book is an exploration of what that means not only for its creator but for the increasing number of such architects of digital environs, all of whom may be charting a new way to design this open-endedness. To capture more powerfully this activity of contriving a complex space for human use, we might even take a cue from the original Latin verb use and say "to architect." This practice of architecture embraces an approach to control that trades the promise of total order for a different ethical position, one that attempts, imperfectly, to reject top-down decision-making in favor of embracing the indeterminate outcomes of social complexities. What is more, this commitment applied as much to Linden Lab's making of their own organization as to their making of Second Life. And in this ongoing predicament they are not alone in high-tech circles; Google, as recent coverage by several journalists has revealed (Carr 2007), is similarly shaped by an attitude that combines a deep faith in technology with a rejection of vertical authority.

In discussing this issue of intentionally limiting control, by a company of its product and of itself, I favor the term "governance" over "management" throughout this work. There are three primary reasons for this. First, management carries with it an enormous weight of past literature on business that tends to portray management as a top-down, strategically implemented project. By contrast, I locate the approach to governance that characterizes Linden Lab as an outgrowth of a historically located point of view, one that in a way explicitly rejects "management" in the traditional business sense. Second, and more important, the ways in which Linden Lab (and other companies like it) are coming to shape the human experience of the digital calls for a term that points to the full range of political and other implications of their position. In seeking to contain and benefit from implementing a mix of regulation and affordances over many users' everyday experience, these companies have left management of a product (or a company) behind and entered the realm of social policy. Finally, governance is a term that can allow us to talk about how such policy must recognize a balance between efforts to control and sources of novelty, in much the same way that, for example, copyright law was built on the attempt to strike a balance between regulating private interest and fostering public innovation (Malaby 2006a; see also Burke 2004).

This is an ethnographic account of the peculiar relationship Linden Lab has to its creation and the implications of this relationship for Linden Lab itself. While initial social science attention has been on the human activity *within* virtual worlds, this work explores one site of their production, with a specific focus on the changing nature of authority and architected disorder within it. The hope is that as a result we will be in a better position to understand the emerging institutions that are ever more able to shape and govern our increasingly digital lives. It explores how an organization that set out to create a deeply and complexly contingent environment is then itself remade by its creation through that domain's emergent effects, in a constantly reiterative process, but without losing its position of greatest influence. These effects continued to shape both Linden Lab's ideals and their practice and set off a spiral of outcomes that continues to this moment. Responding to these eventualities was a constant challenge for Linden Lab, and Lindens displayed a number of responses to it, including seeing themselves as providing value-neutral tools, relying on aesthetically driven appeals rather than rational ones, and turning to the techniques and principles of games and game design to try to manage open-endedness. Linden Lab's struggle to reach an accommodation among its values, its governance of itself, and its governance of its creation may signal the new form of institutions for the digital age, one characterized by something other than the ideal of total control.

The Lindens recognized that new technologies would reconfigure the possible actions that people can take (as they open certain improvisational possibilities and close others); that is, new technologies provide distinct *affordances* to their users. In this, the Lindens are not alone. The history of modern social thought is to a great extent the history of bureaucratic institutions and their changing relationship to human experience. A large part of this is the issue of how bureaucratic institutions govern, often at least in part through technology. Max Weber (1946) and Michel Foucault (1976), most notably, charted the consequences of the rise of practical techniques and representational strategies by which institutions rationalize, discipline, and control. Initial reactions to the implications of new digital affordances (here, principally, vast computing power, mobile devices, and networked technologies) leaned toward the utopian. New technologies, in this technological determinist view, rather than reconfiguring what *might* happen, would inevitably shape our future and, in most accounts, lead to the evaporation of bureaucratic institutions.

But it is by now apparent that institutions are by no account withering away in the wake of these transformations. That is not to say, however, that they are not changing (Kitchin and Dodge 2006, Braman 2007). Programmers and call center employees working in India for a U.S. company are controlled largely through code (see Lessig 1999), in what might be the antithesis of Linden Lab and its approach to Second Life. The programmers' daily lives, including their hours of sleep and work, are thoroughly governed through nonnegotiable code—it controls their login times, implacably measures their error rates, and leaves them "out of sync" with local (Indian) time and its daily rhythms (Aneesh 2006). Here the promise of perfect order is alive and well, but it relies more and more on governance through (software) architecture and less and less on other modes, such as legalistic regulation or shared convention. We see this too in the governance of airports through a combination of software-based and conventional architectural techniques that geographers Rob Kitchin and Martin Dodge (2006) call code/space.

Such continued uses of what we may call the modern approach to governance, even given the innovations to it that software brings, seem more the exception than the rule, however. At Xerox, for instance, attempts to bolster the repair rates of its photocopier technicians through a sizable investment in a new and extensive manual of step-by-step procedures failed quite spectacularly. Rates improved only after they implemented a suggestion made by Julian Orr, an ethnographer looking at work practices within the company, that they support the technicians' emergent practice of sharing "war stories" (Orr 1996). Other ethnographic accounts of emerging technology have similarly conveyed the importance of recognizing how indeterminate the outcomes are of encounters between new technologies and preexisting practice and meanings. Gary Lee Downey (1998), for instance, has charted the unanticipated ways in which students trained in CAD/CAM systems in the United States in the late 1980s were themselves transformed in the way they saw the world. This leaves us in a position where uncovering a determinative account of how these innovations came to be is impossible, such as in Rabinow's (1996) account of the invention of the polymerase chain reaction.

In such work we find a commitment to seeing technology not only beyond how it is situated in specific institutional domains (such as medicine or science) but also beyond its role as simply serving the interests of these domains. We see how technology is more and more directly confronting human sociality, with effects that are not determined by either existing social patterns or the impact of the new. It is particularly important to pursue this line of inquiry as technology increasingly saturates our everyday experience. Take, for example, the many-to-many quality (at least, for those connected) that enables current communication technologies to confound existing institutional controls. This development sparks new and collaborative uses, many of them quite challenging to established interests (the rise of YouTube being a current example). The extent to which this set of expectations shapes broad cultural attitudes in Second Life is extensively documented by Tom Boellstorff, who usefully identifies it as a form of "creationist capitalism" (2008: 100, 206–209), and the question of value in virtual worlds is central to understanding what is happening there. What is the (institutional) business model for new circumstances in which users expect to contribute to the practice of shopping or of entertainment or of diagnosis (to name just a few) while believing that they are unconstrained even in how they craft themselves? This is a question not only for businesses. Similar questions must be asked by other institutions: what is the governance model or the activism model or the learning model under these new circumstances? There has, as ever, been no shortage of eager companies attempting to forge a significant piece of the "digital society." In doing so, they answer some of these questions through the practical development of new digital forms, but virtual worlds are a segment that has brought the deepest of these issues into specific relief and provide a source of key insight for the nature of institutional techniques (and, indeed, viability) to come.

What makes virtual worlds so valuable for answering these questions? First, many virtual worlds are game spaces, where foundational game objectives structure much (though not all) of the human action within them. Early successes such as Ultima Online, Lineage, and Everquest gave way to the current giant in this area: World of Warcraft.[7] World of Warcraft now claims ten million active subscribers (grouped in thousands over multiple, identical servers, each with a complete iteration of the game's world). The sheer numbers involved (both demographically and financially) demand an accounting, in the broad sense, of this new phenomenon, but some of the most significant developments in these kinds of virtual worlds tend to be obscured by the focus on their increasing size. These game-based virtual worlds are giving rise to *guilds*, influential player-made institutions which now span virtual worlds and exert considerable influence over both players' and game makers' actions (Malone 2007). Furthermore, these spaces and their effects—such as the appearance of stable markets in their currencies, objects, and characters (Castronova 2005)—have begun to challenge popular conceptions of what games *are*. Together these developments suggest that we are only beginning to understand the role of games in social life in the current era. Game makers themselves are already confronting how the sometimes surprising social effects that games generate have a significant impact on how they run their games, as Timothy Burke (2004) has written with respect to the changing nature of sovereignty for virtual world makers.

The second thread that we can tease out for why virtual worlds have vaulted onto the scene seems, initially at least, to be in essence quite different. This is the increasing and innovative *uses* of virtual worlds, most obvious in the "social" ones like Second Life. It is Second Life's broader uses for therapy, learning, and commerce that have brought it the lion's share of attention from the media and others in recent years. And in a way this fascination would appear to live up to Linden Lab's own aspirations for Second Life as seen even in its name—one's *Second Life* is intended to be as complete and equivalent an alternative to one's "First Life" as its name would suggest.[8] But these two threads that have caught popular attention (the vast size and increased participation in online games and the innovative "nongame" uses of social virtual worlds) are, I contend, closely related. To see why requires us to approach games differently—specifically, we must recognize that what makes games compelling is not their separateness from our everyday experience but their similarity to it, the way that games present an engaging mixture of pattern and unpredictability that challenges us to act, but also, perhaps, to fail. In games it is a contrived mixture, to be sure, but in short, as game makers have continued to make more and more complex games, they have opened the scope of action within them so broadly as to approach ever more closely the texture of everyday experience. To recognize this, it is also crucial not to see in games only their structures, their rules. Games are not reducible to their rules (Malaby 2007a) but instead legitimize and incorporate forms of contingency that are vital for helping us understand why these architected domains can be a site for the assumption and valorization of intentional self-creation.

This breadth of affordances in virtual worlds owes a great deal to their gameness, so what accounts for this explosion of uses in Second Life and spaces like it is therefore not so removed from what drives the growth of the enormous virtual worlds like World of Warcraft. These worlds share a great deal in the practice of their production, shaped as it is by a combination of game design, computer game development, and software development generally. In their products, these combine to create persistent spaces where users feel a relatively large degree of freedom. But that apparent freedom belies a significant innovation in techniques of governance. In better understanding how these worlds are made and maintained, we might be surprised to find the beginnings of new institutional techniques in the nature of game design itself, which allows game features to be incorporated into the architecture of spaces that become importantly *gamelike*, if not foundationally games. In future inquiry into these spaces, it is vital that we keep in mind the architected nature of virtual worlds, how they achieve their gamelike open-endedness, and the ethical implications of those facts for the changing human relationship to institutions in the digital age.[9]

Let us turn back, then, to the earlier notion that in important ways these games, and the gamelike virtual worlds built on their principles, exist counter to bureaucracy—in the classical sense—and its close ties to the most explicit ideals of modernity. As *socially legitimate spaces for cultivating the unexpected* (Malaby 2007a), games and the virtual worlds based on them can usefully be thought of as the mirror of bureaucracy. If bureaucracy is driven by an ethic of determinacy or *necessity* and aspires to eliminate the exceptional case, games and virtual worlds are driven by an ethic of *contingency*; that is, they are places where the unexpected is supposed to happen.[10] Of course, bureaucracy *in practice* is also a site for contingency (and regularity). Bureaucratic projects certainly do not perfectly realize the modern aim of eliminating the uncalled-for. The point, however, is that bureaucratic projects, such as Xerox's initial efforts mentioned above, or those of the companies that Aneesh describes, *aspire* to reduce contingency—that is the ideal. For Weber and those who have followed his thought, this is no less than one of the central cultural ideals of modernity. With it we have seen, especially for the nation-state, attempts to maintain this order through portraits of an imagined collective life that obscure idiosyncratic practice (see Herzfeld 1993). Games, by contrast, are socially legitimate domains where unpredictable events are *supposed to happen*, and that is why their rise suggests a changing relationship between institutions and the rationalizing techniques (and strategic representations) that have served them so well in the past.

One aim of this work is to bring games into our conversation about what is happening not only in our relationship to technology but to governance in all the domains in which it is found. At the same time that games have made their presence increasingly impossible to ignore, much of game studies scholarship was long mired in competing, formalist approaches (loosely labeled as narratology and ludology), which shared unproductive root assumptions about the structure of games in all times and places and tended to assume that games are intrinsically set apart from everyday life (this is due in large part to the long-standing and unexamined association of games with play; see Malaby 2007a for a full discussion of this issue). But this self-ghettoization of game studies is ending as a new wave of scholars has found it productive to forge new ground in our understanding of games.[11] Games at this very moment are being incorporated into more and more domains of experience, and excellent work in this vein has begun to appear.[12] A leading example is the work of the journalist Julian Dibbell (2006), who has gone the furthest in suggesting that, by eroding the culturally robust (for the West) separation of work and play, the advent of games' ubiquity in workers'/players' daily experience may herald the beginnings of what he calls ludo-capitalism. In a similar vein, this book explores the point of view of those who are integrating elements from game making into their creations and even their own institutions in ways that appear to move beyond the bureaucratic logic by which those spaces have worked in the past. The central puzzle is one of Linden Lab's own governance, even while that conundrum also characterizes its challenges vis-à-vis Second Life. In making Second Life's world, Linden Lab's world was continually remade.

The book charts how, in setting out to make a world that is supposed to make itself (through the content-generating actions of its users), Linden Lab evinced a remarkable and antibureaucratic commitment to unintended consequences, and then found itself shaped by Second Life as the world and its effects grew.[13] Making it up as they went along, Linden Lab's original ethical attitudes (in practice and discourse) toward people and technology were subtly changed but not necessarily overturned, and this challenges our previously held ideas about institutions and their relationship to what they create. Above all, this underscores for us the importance of understanding the power of the deep architectural position of the relatively small number of people and organizations at the forefront of constructing the digital societies to come. Furthermore, the designers of digital space are shaped by a set of ideas about technology and authority that continue to resonate throughout the halls of Silicon Valley. I term this distinctive combination of distrust of vertical authority, faith in technology, and faith in the legitimacy of emergent effects as "technoliberalism," which marks both its similarities to neoliberal thought but also its emphasis on contriving complex systems through the manipulation of technology. Organizations shaped by this view, in their struggles to act and preserve their position relative to their creations, are working out new institutional techniques to cultivate the indeterminacy previously anathema to organizations. They do so in part because of a faith that inheres in this outlook—that open-ended practice, in the aggregate, will produce not only things of value (an economy) but emergent patterns that will lead to social goods writ large. The challenge, from this point of view, is how to contrive such contingency. The people of Linden Lab, remarkably, out of accident, ambition, or necessity sought to embrace this conundrum practically and thus began a very bumpy ride at the edge of their own institutional existence.

1_THE PRODUCT

Second Life, Capital, and the Possibility
of Failure in a Virtual World

Sitting at a free desk in Linden Lab's Second Street offices, I have just finished some work on my avatar, ending up with some slightly spiky red hair that I like and a frame more human than superhuman (though perhaps a touch more trim than my own). A Linden on the QA (quality assurance) team walks by, and I catch his attention to point proudly at my handiwork. "Very nice," he says, "but, my friend, you need clothes." I look at my avatar. It is (I am) not naked; I am wearing the jeans that one begins one's Second Life wearing, and a T-shirt I picked up at a special event a few days before, with the name of the dance club on it. "What do you mean?" I ask, perplexed. "Look," he says, "let me tell you a few places that sell *good* clothes, you know what I'm sayin'? Now, let's start with what you want. What look are you going for?" Feeling that I had fallen into the deep and treacherous waters of fashion, I hemmed for a moment before mentioning that I admired the crisply tailored white suit that the avatar of Wagner James Au (then-"embedded" journalist at Linden Lab) wore. "I know someone who makes *gorgeous* suits," he answered, "Now here's where you go." Shortly thereafter, and a couple of thousand L$ poorer, my avatar sported a beige linen suit, complete with white dress shirt and stylish red and teal tie, along with sunglasses whose lenses could change color at a command and teal sneakers, to make the look just a touch more casual. "There. Now you're ready to be seen," he said, and headed back to his desk.

The bulk of media attention that Second Life and other virtual worlds have received has concerned the surprising "reality" of their markets, the way they generate goods that are exchanged for familiar currencies (or for local, virtual world currencies that can themselves be bought and sold in currency markets; Castronova 2005, Lastowka and Hunter 2003). Trade in virtual items is still a new idea for some, but it should not be as unfamiliar as it may seem. After all, many people regularly pay for items that have no tangible existence, such as mobile phone accounts or downloaded computer software. The items in Second Life are in this respect no different, but what makes things a bit more complicated is the fact that almost everything you can buy in Second Life, at least at first glance, can only be used *in* Second Life. (Interesting exceptions include PDF files, which can be printed out, and images or video files, which can be distributed beyond Second Life quite easily).

This might lead some to think of the objects in Second Life as more like tokens in a game than valued possessions, things that are owned by the venue owner, like the putters at a miniature golf course. According to this view, users of these virtual worlds are players, effectively renting use of the in-game objects, which must then be returned. But there are a number of reasons why such objects accumulate "real" value in Second Life, and this changes the attitudes of users to "their" stuff. We can recognize why this is so by beginning simply with the fact that these objects and other things, like Second Life, persist. Access to them by the user persists as well, and in this sense they are a resource for that user's action in Second Life. What is more, these objects can have different properties that shape this social use. The creator of something has a number of options available when making an object. It can be set as copyable or not copyable, modifiable (meaning others with a copy of it or the original can change it) or unmodifiable, and transferable or nontransferable. For transferable objects, a price can be set, and sellers can in fact set their stores up as virtual vending machines, requiring no one on-site to make their sales. I bought my suit by right-clicking on a picture of the suit and then selecting "Purchase." So the first thing we must understand about virtual world economies like that of Second Life is that they have all the necessary elements to support trade: alienable goods, a currency, and (most important) persistence (this persistence need not be guaranteed—like a frontier economy, it need only be sure enough for some to "bet" on).

My next encounter with what this means in practice came in one of my early explorations of Second Life after buying my first land. Having upgraded my account from the one-time fee version (US$9.95—later this basic subscription became completely free) to the monthly subscription (US$9.95 per month), I enjoyed some of the benefits of a "premium" account, including the right to own land, and I shopped around until I found a small plot on the corner of one of the many squares that make up the "grid" of Second Life. Each of these squares is called a "sim" (short for simulator) and each corresponds to an actual server that controls that square. The servers, like those of many Internet companies) are housed at a high-security and temperature-controlled "co-location" or "colo," a separate building in which Linden Lab rents space for its servers. On a visit there in 2005 I stood before the racks and racks of servers on which all the data for Second Life sat and marveled at the disjunction between the cramped, warm space in which I stood and the wide open, and often somewhat empty, vistas of Second Life.

My plot of land had (and has) a beautiful vista: a nice water view (waterfront properties in Second Life, as offline, are always more valuable). With an effective size of 512 square meters, this is not a large piece of Second Life, by any stretch, but it was big enough that I began to think that I ought to put something on it—a place where I could invite others to sit down for a chat. And here again we confront what is strangely familiar yet unfamiliar about Second Life. What does it mean to sit down in Second Life? It means that you sit your avatar (your virtual body) down, and the object you sit on (if it is programmed be sat on) will actually contain a bit of software that tells your avatar *how* to sit, whether to lounge, to sit upright, to cross your legs, or what have you.

Much of the conversation in Second Life in 2005 (long before the ability to speak in Second Life and hear others was introduced) was text-based "chat," typed comments that were visible to every avatar close enough to "hear" them.[1] In thinking about providing a social space on my land, I had already learned (from my own interactions with other users) that sitting down was preferred for this kind of conversation—perhaps it was the familiar sight lines, or the familiar arrangement of virtual bodies that suggested intimacy and focused attention. As many scholars who have spent time in virtual worlds have noted (Castronova 2005, Dibbell 2006, and Taylor 2006, to name a few), it takes little time for a user to identify strongly with his or her avatar. With it you can take meaningful actions in the virtual world and, more important, you can fail while trying. It may seem a bit strange for me to tie these two things together—meaning and failure—and even to discuss failure in Second Life at all. With no preset goals, what is failure in Second Life?

To answer this question we should begin by recognizing the place of failure in our everyday social experience. As the sociologist Erving Goffman showed (1959), the way we present ourselves is always related to the particular domain in which we act, and furthermore, we seek to put forth certain impressions while avoiding others. A server in a fine restaurant manages the front of the house like a stage set (Goffman's "frontstage"), protecting from view or other discernment any messy contingencies that may befall the "backstage" (for an extended discussion of this from an insider's perspective, see Bourdain 2007: 64–74; see also Fine 1996). At a job interview, the applicant strives to project a specific version of his or her self, one that is an apt fit with the open position. Social differentiation (status) trades to a certain extent on those who can perform these roles with élan, and it is the possibility of failure that makes success meaningful (and vice versa); thus are the culturally "competent" (and this often informs class differences) separable from those that are, well, not. Social expectations for successful performance are ever-present (Bauman 1977), even when there are no

Figure 1. My Second Life home, complete with sitting area (below the "hammered copper" dome), and with the Second Life sun setting. Another user's home sits in the background to the right.

specific goals; often the only goal is to be seen as a competent member of a social group in the circumstances at hand.

In Second Life, not to have a social space of this sort risked such failure for me. By having one, I would be more likely to present myself as a knowledgeable, competent user of Second Life—something other than a "newbie" (or "noob"; see Boellstorff 2008: 72–75, 134–136). I found a nice, towerlike structure from a "free content" area (a place where other users drop modifiable objects that others can grab copies of for free) and proceeded to tweak it (and my land) a bit until I had a nice bridge attached to a domed sitting area on the top of the tower (see figure 1).

Now I could invite others to my land and appear the thoughtful (or at least minimally competent) host. I could respond proudly to inquiries about how I managed to make the roof appear to be hammered copper by alluding to creative use of a Spanish-tile texture, wrapping one tile over the entirety of the dome (in fact, this happy outcome was very much an accident—I expected to see a full-fledged tile roof when I applied the texture). It is Second Life's persistence *and* its open-endedness (here, the possibility of failure, or accidental success) that makes it possible for this kind of specific local meaning to accumulate there. Later in the book I connect these features of Second Life to what it owes to games, but here I would like to focus on what the presence of success and failure mean for the stakes of Second Life. Its users are playing not just a game with borrowed tokens that will eventually end but a never-ending game with tokens they make themselves. That this could just as well characterize other domains of our lives is exactly the point.

(-: :-)

Computer games pioneered the avatar and a particular interface for its mastery, one that by convention involves the combined use of a QWERTY keyboard for movement and a mouse for adjusting what you see and how you interact with objects/other avatars. Alongside this development came a number of other features of 3-D online environments and the objects within them: the apparent physics by which these objects and avatars interact, as well as the idea of persistence, whereby user actions can make durable (if limited) changes to the game world.

What drove this innovation in computer games? All games make performative (in the Austinian sense; Austin 1975) demands on their players—actions they must master (along with guesses they must successfully make) to accomplish game objectives. This is one respect in which games are open-ended in a way quite similar to Second Life—at any given moment, things may turn out one way or the other. They are, to use the philosophical term, *contingent* (as opposed to *necessary* or determined). This performative contingency of avatars—the never-perfect mastery of a body analogue through a refined interface of fine-motor skills—is a crucial part of Second Life, and something that helps us account for why it feels like "play" or a "game" to many of its users. This is because *it is possible to fail*, and to fail quite visibly and in multiple ways, when acting within Second Life. This contingent performance begins with mastery of one's avatar, often in view of others. And unlike in many other domains of online interaction, such as those that are primarily text-based, the scope for failure is much wider, containing text performance (in chat or instant messaging [IM]) along with avatar presentation and competence. In its physics, avatar affordances, and persistence, Second Life therefore owes an enormous amount to computer games.

Second Life's open-endedness, the way it is a fertile landscape for new uses, is inextricably linked to the experience of being in Second Life as someone who must perform through an avatar and is aware that one might fail in doing so, even in mundane ways (such as accidentally toggling off while flying, leading to an embarrassing fall, complete with an animation of limbs flailing). One soon realizes that, in many of the other actions one takes in Second Life, one is similarly called upon to perform in what feels like a social game. One of my first tasks as a new user was to "make" myself—shape my avatar via a complex set of "tools" for managing everything from my jaw width to my waist height—knowing all the while that this would be my presentation of self to others in Second Life, with whatever judgments of competence that might entail. It was at the conclusion of this process, having considered my work on my appearance done, that I showed it off proudly to the passing Linden, only to be whisked along on a shopping spree.

Thus there is urgency to much of the performance in Second Life, quite similar to that which characterizes language immersion. A user is driven to master movement, chat, building, flying, and other skills to a great extent because of the contestation over performance that characterizes games, in a contrived fashion, and everyday life, in a boundless fashion. But Second Life, although "boundless" in its open-endedness in the same way that other aspects of life are (there are no shared and established game objectives), is more like games in one important respect: it is an environment that is subject to the contrivance of its makers, who have leveraged these elements from games to make something that can compel involvement (Calleja 2007) and effectively begin to approach the texture of everyday life.

This performative and social, gamelike quality to Second Life not only forms the foundation of its scope for failure and success but also points the way toward a better understanding of the bases of trust. Goffman is again helpful, as he recognized how groups that seek to maintain an impression together (a "team") themselves generate and depend on trust—trust that the frontstage will be maintained. As current research on online games has shown, collaborative action in urgent conditions is highly generative of trust and belonging (Ducheneaut, Moore, and Nickell 2007). This point should not really surprise us; teams build trust through a combination of interaction that is sufficiently high in bandwidth and oriented toward a common objective amid uncertain circumstances. Trust is something that many games (those that allow for teamwork) are contrived to accomplish, and the lesson to take from them is that a sufficient scope for social action, beyond the textual or aural, becomes fertile ground for social bonds *because* of the broad range of small to large acts of coordination (of bodies, of avatars) that take place within them, any one of which may succeed or fail. Much like a dance, then, avatar-mediated interaction can become a source of trust that builds over time, not simply because of the prospects for successful coordination but because of the multiple small moments of success and failure, and not just with direct reference to the explicit aim at hand. The mutual coordination of performance in Second Life extends to the most mundane practices of managing avatar distance, sight lines, posture, and the like. It is through this emergent practice, as an arena where some are masters and some are learning, that trust is generated, and this means the generation of one component of the stakes in Second Life: social capital.

Capital in Play

It is tempting to account for the breadth of creative action in spaces like Second Life by citing the effective removal of certain constraints, such as the constraining effects of geography (Ondrejka 2007). In this way, freedom is associated with creativity and, in fact, with the *absence* of stakes. Although there are understandable reasons why we might look at virtual worlds and see them as places that have so radically reduced certain kinds of costs that they are effectively consequence-free (and that this therefore accounts for why people do creative things there), this is an error. Failure to present myself properly (or host visitors properly) in Second Life had consequences, as my QA friend underscored. To understand these consequences, we should be ready to look more closely and recognize how the stakes in virtual worlds are not eliminated but instead radically *reconfigured* as compared to most other domains. It is this realignment of resources and constraints that may account for the stakes that virtual worlds have generated.

Virtual worlds do transform and vastly reduce many of the material costs of the virtual commodities produced within them as compared to their offline analogues; specifically, those associated with production and distribution (any Second Life object is near-instantly replicable code). But there is always a temptation, on seeing the ways in which virtual worlds seem to collapse geography in this way, to see this reduction as removing constraints altogether. The radical reduction in material costs can lead us to think that a place like Second Life is effectively a post-scarcity economy. But this conclusion is actually only the result of a long-ingrained habit of thinking of the economy as constituted and bounded by the market, a habit to which many decades of academic treatment have contributed.

Scholarship, however, has slowly come to reflect more closely the human experience of the economy and has developed a picture of it that incorporates not only the ways material resources (cash, commodities) accumulate and move about through market exchange, but also how other resources are accumulated and circulate, such as through reciprocity, the source of social capital (trust), as well as learning and authorization, the sources of cultural capital.[2] As most social actors recognize, we frequently parlay one of these kinds of resources into another. We may invest market capital in learning (tuition), social capital to find a job, or cultural competence to establish networks of reciprocity (through hosting a dinner party, for example). For Pierre Bourdieu, human practice over time accumulates in these different forms, whether in the congealed labor of commodities, the lasting obligations of social networks, or the established cultural practices of taste (Bourdieu 1986). All these resources accumulate over time; human effort congeals in these various kinds of capital that then become the resources available to us as we seek to accomplish our daily objectives. To put it another way, human capital is the first resource for people, and with its application over time it generates material, social, and cultural capital.

What does this mean for virtual worlds? The first thing we must notice is that their structural characteristics of persistence and open-endedness (contingency) make the accumulation of these forms of capital just as possible within them as they are elsewhere. Goods (with vastly reduced production and distribution costs, it is true), human relationships, and skills can be created and obtained in virtual worlds as a result of the expending of effort over time, assuming such effort is successful. Whatever the reconfiguration or reduction in material production and distribution costs, trust and competence, at least, continue to be scarce commodities in virtual worlds, because social failure is an ever-present possibility. Establishing and maintaining a network of trust and obligation does not become a trivial exercise simply because many of the material costs of communication are lowered. Similarly, gaining competencies that can be applied toward innovation is also not a costless (or even near-costless) transaction. This is because reciprocity and learning, as forms of human exchange, have always required time in a way that isolated market transactions, over and done with as they often aspire to be, do not.

We are better able to account for the stakes of virtual worlds when we see them as reconfiguring the relationships among these kinds of resources and putting them at risk to be gained or lost on the basis of successful or failing social action. It may be accurate to say that, over much of history, market capital has dominated other forms of human exchange precisely because of the high costs of producing and transporting material goods, and that therefore virtual worlds bring this situation more into balance (at least for those with the material resources to access them!) by elevating the impact of reciprocity and learning, so that all these forms of exchange are on a par with one another. But each of these forms of capital develop in virtual worlds with certain distinctive features, and examining them further gives us insight not only into what is at stake in places like Second Life, but also how the architecture of virtual worlds can shape this production of value.

Market Capital

The most familiar form of capital, market capital tends to be both durable and transferable, existing in the form of goods and services (commodities) or currency. But the power of market capital lies in its capacity to be re-exchanged, achieved most fully in the form of currency. Market capital, unlike other forms, enables exchanges that are immediate and isolated, demanding no corresponding moral exchange (reciprocity) or cultural exchange (learning and authorization), although these other dimensions are often present. In its ideal form, then, market capital is a resource that can be drawn on in isolation from one's connections (one's social capital) or one's credentials and competencies, beyond the minimum cultural competencies required by the market itself. In this respect, success and failure tend to be less of a defining feature of market transactions—they are done, and it matters little if they are done well or poorly.

Commodities

Virtual worlds have surprised many with the degree to which they generate tradable goods that can now be found easily through online markets (eBay, IGE). While the lack of tangibility to these goods makes some of those unfamiliar with virtual worlds initially hesitant to accord them equal status with offline goods, it should take only a moment's consideration to render such reactions untenable as a basis for analytical distinctions. The purchase of goods that we durably own but which are intangible applies equally well to such items as software, telecom accounts, ringtones, and other elements of digital life that people rely on around the world. F. Gregory Lastowka and Dan Hunter (2003), writing from a legal point of view, have demonstrated that both normatively and descriptively these goods must be considered property, and this signals a larger trend where the status of information as a commodity is becoming undeniable.

Initial skepticism may also be colored by a suspicion that these virtual commodities are, like the worlds themselves, somehow not serious or worthwhile. Whether these goods are frivolous, however, is a normative question, and in any case it is one that presupposes the very distinction—that these are worlds without consequences, as opposed to the "real world" with its consequences—that the reality of virtual world economies should help us overcome. In any case, commodities are the most obvious instance of the exchange of value across worlds, as they are widely available for purchase through simple credit-card transactions. Buyers thus convert their market capital (in the form of currency or credit) into market capital in the form of commodities, virtual goods. They make the conversion not simply within the world's economy but across the world's economy and the national economy of their currency. (This is analogous to the purchase over the Internet of goods from another country.)

But the most important feature of virtual world commodities is the possibility of transforming the costs of producing or distributing them. Instead of letting the code-based environment dictate easy replicability, many virtual worlds have *imposed* scarcity, such that acquiring, making, or developing things of value demands significant amounts of time and most objects of value cannot easily be duplicated. This tends to be true for those virtual worlds that are foundationally games (MMORPGs), such as World of Warcraft. As a result, the values for these commodities can bear a strong relationship to the amount of time required to make or acquire each item. These efforts to control scarcity on the part of the worlds' makers are not immutable—players with the right access (perhaps by drawing on social capital) or abilities (cultural capital) can hack or exploit under certain circumstances; this is just one more way that these domains exhibit their complexity—they cannot be perfectly governed.

Also at play here is the use value of the item; that is, what it allows you to do, whether as a marker of status, an element of in-game combat, or otherwise. This value, the product of the item's supply and demand, can be exploited by those who acquire or make goods for sale by the application of cultural capital in the form of skill or credentials necessary or helpful (in terms of minimizing time) to acquire the item, by the application of social capital (connections) to locate the item, and so forth. That difference—that is, how much easier it is for someone to acquire or make an item more efficiently than a prospective buyer—is what the seller depends on to make a profit. This virtual world entrepreneurship has been most fully explored by Julian Dibbell (2006).

So in the generation of these commodities we already see multiple kinds of resources in play, as players in MMORPGs leverage them to generate commodities that can be exchanged for currency. It is also worth noting that the distribution costs are in any case transformed, as the virtual nature of the commodities makes their transfer relatively easy, although this result depends as well on the architecture of the virtual world itself. Can items, for example, be sent via asynchronous communication (such as e-mail) from one account to another? Must this be done within the world? Even more interesting is to consider the limits of the objects' use value. Can we imagine that some of them could be "used" outside their original domains? What are the consequences of someone posting screen shots or other "proof" of ownership of an item to personal blogs and photo sharing sites? To what extent are items constrained by the "story" of the world from which they originate?

Second Life and other creations like it (ActiveWorlds, There) are different on this point, with important consequences for the configuration of these forms of capital. In these worlds the (re)production and distribution costs of creating items are both drastically reduced. Let us recall that Second Life in particular is built on the premise that users make their own content, and that they furthermore own the intellectual property rights to whatever they make. The permissions (for copying, transfer, and the like) for objects made in Second Life are set by their

maker (or anyone with access to a modifiable object). Thus in Second
Life not only is it extraordinarily inexpensive to distribute items, but
also their duplication costs can be near zero as well. As a result, the
investment of time and effort involved designing and (initially) making
in-world commodities has a disproportionate weight for these virtual
world commodities. One implication of this is a suggestion that "creativity" is the preeminent source of value in Second Life—it is the
scarce commodity (see Boellstorff 2008: 205–236). This returns us to
the core issue of success and failure. Any user can design a new T-shirt
in Second Life, but what makes one design a success and another a
failure? The right product, as in offline fashion, must tweak existing
forms in just the right direction, resonating with potential buyers, each
of whom is eager to distinguish him- or herself from what has come
before with an eye-catching new look.

In the Second Life fashion designer and the Second Life consumer
we find a meeting point of performances, and mutual success brings
capital to them both, at least until that look itself has become tired. In
some ways, it is the deeply fashion-oriented economy of Second Life
that argues most strongly for the "success" of Linden Lab's attempt to
recreate "First Life." It is here that we must confront how the value of
commodities can rely as much on a set of cultural meanings in addition
to the factors heretofore described. A common example is that of the
baseball card; its value accumulates relative to the cultural importance
placed on such objects, which elevates some materially nearly worth-
less items to an exalted status as "memorabilia" or the like. As outlined
below, this is a particular form of cultural capital, its objectified state,
but I foreshadow that discussion here because cultural capital is con-
ventionally parlayed into market capital through events such as assess-
ments and appraisals, which themselves depend on a combination of
scarcity and meaning. We might then ask: If the cultural capital of
meaningful objects is generated in virtual worlds, how are these forms
of nostalgic or innovative value supported or undermined by the nature of virtual items as potentially replicable code themselves?

There is a further wrinkle to understanding commodities in virtual
worlds: How are services to be understood? Are they a form of market

capital? Services are highly commodified, but they are not durable and transferable in the ways that most commodities or currencies are. They appear to be a direct application of cultural capital (expertise), rather than the accumulation of human capital that we see in goods, virtual or otherwise. Nonetheless, services are a form of market capital because what is purchased is the labor and expertise of one or more others as delimited by time. Purveyors of services sell their time, and hence make a direct parlay of their embodied cultural capital, acquired in human effort over time, into market capital, the application of cultural capital in time. The distinguishing feature of market capital transactions still remains; the service transaction is minimally possible without any necessary elements of moral obligation (reciprocity) or learning and authorization.

There are a number of services sold in virtual worlds, such as notary services, design consultations, writing services, and (in World of Warcraft) enchanting and lockpicking. Here, as in offline experience, the conversion of cultural capital, in the form of both competencies and credentials, into market capital is accomplished by applying those competencies through time, and that application of competencies in the service is the exchangeable commodity, the market capital. A number of important questions remain: How are emerging or existing means to display competence and credentials involved in service providers' efforts in the marketplace? Do services, so closely tied to competence and credentials, rely also more heavily on social capital; that is, are social networks, as opposed to advertising and other forms, particularly good paths to potential customers? In all these dimensions, how does the architecture of virtual worlds specifically shape these practices?

Currency

Currency is market capital in its most liquid form: highly transformable, frequently anonymous, and productive of immediate exchanges that most clearly suggest no moral relationship (Parry and Bloch 1989). Unlike commodities, which have a use value, currency has value only in its exchange for other currencies, commodities, or when parlayed into other forms. Many theorists have noted that as a phenomenon money is ultimately and peculiarly reliant on a shared sense of trust, and many of the ingredients of this trust are deeply practical.[3] Common practical knowledge and use of currency provides one part of the foundation required for any money to be "real" and to represent and store "real" value (Dominguez 1990). Unlike commodities, then, currency has long been embedded in the mundane practices of person-to-person transactions, involving verification both of the currency itself and of the transaction (ensuring correct amounts, change, and proper application of things like taxes and fees). In the absence of many of these features of cash transactions in virtual worlds, how is collective trust in currency established?

This transition in the foundations of trust in currency from the mundane to the virtual is already under way for conventional currencies. The establishment of the euro is a particularly apt case that illuminates the position of virtual currencies. The euro was a fascinating, and perhaps unprecedented, instance where the introduction of a virtual currency not only preceded its physical rollout but was deemed a necessary test of the currency's viability (Malaby 2003b). This reversal reflected an important landmark in a long transformation in the concept of trustable currency, away from specie and toward an abstract representation of value. For much of the past two centuries, this transformation has hinged on the effectiveness of verifying the physical currency itself and on training citizens to be competent (that is, to have the cultural capital) to verify their currency in the course of face-to-face exchange. With the euro's rollout, the first test of verification of the currency rested not on mundane, unmediated verification by everyday users but instead on the establishment of its value online, in currency markets, where it was available two years before it ever saw the streets.

What does this mean for virtual worlds? It demonstrates that the generation of value for currencies is already resting increasingly not on the physical verification of notes and coins but on the collective trust in networked financial institutions, including currency markets, banks, and transaction verification services (like VeriSign and PayPal). This trust is built, in turn, on a small, wealthy segment of the global population's increasing familiarity with the practices of virtual trade. In short, it demonstrates in a different way why we should not be surprised to see virtual world currencies act like more familiar currencies; after all, the euro itself was virtually real first, and this signals that the very foundations of the peculiar phenomenon of money are shifting further toward the institutional and away from the phenomenological. For virtual worlds, this raises the following questions: What kinds of institutions underwrite virtual currency? Is it the company that makes the world itself, existing banks and other financial institutions, new third party vendors, currency markets, or some combination of all three? How is the relationship of trust necessary for the legitimacy of a currency established among these institutions and between them and the users, and therefore how might we recognize practices of reciprocity in this process? Just as important, how does the architecture of the Internet itself and of particular domains shape users' practices and expectations so as to generate new paths toward legitimacy for lending institutions?

One answer may be found in the establishment of Stagecoach Island, by Wells Fargo Bank, on a private island within Second Life wherein residents could participate in a private economy. According to news.com:[4]

Visitors there can skydive, fly hovercrafts, dance, and shop. But woven into the experience, to which Wells Fargo has been inviting groups of people in San Diego and Austin, Texas, is a series of financial messages intended to help them learn something about money management. . . . Stagecoach Island takes place on several private islands inside Linden Lab's virtual world, "Second Life." But while "Second Life" is open to the public, the Wells Fargo islands are accessible only by those who have received invitations from the bank and, thus, is branded entirely as a Wells Fargo environment. Regular "Second Life" members cannot access Stagecoach Island. . . . Stagecoach Island players are given $30 in imaginary money with which to buy clothes, pay for rides, and the like. The idea, though, is to teach the players to save money—they earn 10 percent per day on "deposits"—and to learn new things about money management through a series of quizzes that, when completed, reward players with $5 of new funds.

By making access to the island, and an allowance in its virtual currency, available for free—or rather, in exchange for contact information—to select young adults, Wells Fargo tried to leverage its cultural capital as a credentialed financial institution with its social capital in its connections to select groups to generate both market capital in the form of new accounts and the cultural capital of the credential of widely acknowledged competence in online finance. The effort was ended after some months, and Wells Fargo moved on to do a similar project in a competitor of Second Life's, There.com. Similar attempts to parlay social capital into market capital and cultural capital, and back again, are prevalent throughout Second Life, whether by corporations, nonprofit and government institutions (such as the National Oceanic and Atmospheric Administration's island), or individual Second Life users.

Social Capital

Social capital is a resource that depends on the special qualities of reciprocity, as first outlined by Marcel Mauss (1967). Unlike immediate and equivalent exchanges, such as those of the market, reciprocal exchanges (in the form of objects, services, expressions of concern, and so forth) imply a moral relationship, where the account is "never settled" among individuals or groups, and success and failure become all the more possible. Central to this phenomenon is time, but in contrast to the commodification via delimited time in the service industry, here time is specifically not delimited: any given exchange continues a relationship into the future, leaving open the possibility of the nature and quality of the next transaction. Over time, social capital is the resource constituted by these relationships, one that can be drawn upon for advice, support, or other resources. As such, social capital must be cultivated, maintained in a way that market capital does not require; here success is measured by the ability to participate in an ongoing exchange of obligations, and failure is either not to return such a concern or favor or to demand too many without return.[5]

Connections

In virtual worlds, social capital is a resource that has garnered increasing attention, primarily with respect to the generation of new social relationships within virtual worlds and with respect to how social ties can bridge within and between virtual worlds and other parts of people's lives (Taylor and Kolko 2003). It is perhaps not surprising then that we are drawn first to identify the familiar social groups within worlds (such as groups in Second Life or guilds in World of Warcraft) or outside them (such as kin networks or peer networks), all of which recreate or draw on conventional forms of social organization. But we thereby pay less attention to the practices of reciprocity that create and sustain these networks. This is unfortunate, because a research focus on the practices of reciprocity in virtual worlds would allow us to see where new forms of social networks are created, even if they are never realized in conventional social forms. I am thinking in particular here of guild structure in conventional MMORPGs, where a form of social organization is written into the code of the world itself, and how focusing on this as the social formation par excellence in World of Warcraft might blind us to other kinds of social networks (such as those associated with World of Warcraft's auction houses, for example). For Second Life, it was the existence of such ongoing relationships between Linden Lab and many of its longtime users that drew critical attention, with a number of users complaining that these users were given special favors and other attention by Linden Lab. One example of this was Linden Lab's support for the user group Bedazzle's attempt to create a game within Second Life. These connected users were labeled the "Feted Inner Core" (FIC for short; see Boellstorff 2008: 226). The Wikipedia entry for Second Life defines the FIC as "a derogatory term for any . . . 'clique' of successful residents on Second Life, especially where such a group is seen as having been granted special favors (by Linden Lab, landowners, or other influential organizations) that maintain its success." As in similar offline charges of cronyism and the like, the moral economy of reciprocity does not simply generate civically healthy social capital (in Putnam's sense [2001]); it always contains as well the possibility of social exclusion. When I was directed by a Linden to one set of stores to outfit my avatar, and not others, who is to say if that kind of guidance bespeaks unfair competition?

The parlay of social capital into other forms is also possible between Second Life and other domains, with a prominent example being the novelist Cory Doctorow's launch of a novel in virtual form within Second Life (Doctorow 2005). Doctorow, with the credentials (a published author) and competence (the ability to write this novel and others and to present his work publicly), made use of his connections with the Second Life community (and one of its primary journalists, Wagner James Au, in particular) to create an event where virtual copies of his book (designed by residents in a competition) were available, and at which he was available to talk about the work and to sign the books (virtually).[6] The Second Life copies of the book were free, so a direct parlay of social and cultural capital into market capital for Doctorow was not the effect, but this does not mean that the event had no consequences in terms of market capital for Doctorow, who argues that such distribution in fact increases his material gain from writing. In any case, the exchange is all the more interesting because market capital was not at its forefront. As in many such events, on- and offline, the conversion of social capital into cultural capital (in the form of status) is the central exchange.

Cultural Capital

Cultural capital is the realization of what a given cultural group finds to be meaningful or important in bodies, objects, and offices. It includes the competencies and credentials that individuals or groups acquire over time within a particular historical context and the objects that become valuable through their association with such meaning. It has three forms: embodied, objectified, and institutionalized (Bourdieu 1986: 243–248). Cultural capital is distinctive for its specificity to a context of meaning and practice, such as contexts associated with nation, class, region, or sources of social separation, and thus its acquisition is not amenable to immediate and isolated transactions. Instead, cultural capital is acquired through the culturally embedded practices of learning, in the informal sense, and authorization, in the official sense. Such exchanges generate a feeling of belonging, of identification with a cultural group. The exception is cultural capital in the objectified form, here termed *artifacts*, where the purchase of such goods does not entail the cultural competence necessary to consume, that is, "appreciate" them.

Competencies (Embodied)

The competencies embodied in individuals as a result of their learning form a basic resource for all human beings. It is the application of this cultural capital in action that enables an individual to engage the world and to interact with others in it, beginning with the basic application of language and gesture but encompassing every other means by which individuals are able to act meaningfully. A very small set of examples includes: making small talk, being literate, hitting a major league curveball, navigating social service bureaucracies, tracking and shooting a deer, tracking and clicking on a target in a networked computer game, typing witty comments quickly in a synchronous chat-based environment, and demonstrating unflappability in the face of unexpected gambling losses.

These competencies are acquired through learning, often in childhood, a practice that involves long-term tutelage under the guidance of either competent others—such as parents, teachers, mentors, or peers—or the objectified cultural knowledge found in objects such as books, tools, built environments, and technology. Cultural competencies are powerful markers of background and are more specifically associated with cultural distinctions such as class, gender, ethnicity, profession, religion, age group, and many more. Jerome Karabel (2005) has documented how over the course of the twentieth century Harvard, Princeton, and Yale developed admissions policies that gathered information to evaluate applicants in terms of a broader array of cultural capital than simply scholastic ability. This allowed them, for example, to slow the rise of successful Jewish entrants over the first half of the twentieth century. By expanding their forms of information gathering and evaluation into such areas as athletic team membership they sought to measure "character," a form of cultural capital that could be relied on as a predictor of future wealth because it excluded those not already enculturated to the relatively ethnically homogenous upper class.

In virtual worlds, we see a scene much more in flux, as the cultural competencies within it are in the process of becoming. As a result, the economy of practices there may not currently, as in Karabel's cases, simply reproduce entrenched socioeconomic differences. Where in virtual worlds, then, are existing competencies finding new purchase, and where are new competencies generated? Although here we might be tempted to identify the avatar as the "actor," the entity that acquires the ability to act competently in places like Second Life, we must keep in mind that cultural competencies are inescapably embodied. The need for a tool or technologically mediated environment (such as the avatar) to utilize some of these competencies does not change this fact, and thus to separate the physical from the avatar is to reintroduce a gap between online and offline that does not exist. More familiar competencies—piloting an airplane, rowing a canoe, handling customer service telephone calls, pedaling a bicycle, or even writing—also require the proper circumstance to be employed, including the requisite technologies and forms of mediation.

If we think of competencies developed within and across virtual worlds, then, as essentially not different from those individually and collectively developed in other domains, we can see more easily how the application of such competencies can itself transcend one domain for another. The influx of corporations and other institutions into Second Life reflects an investment on their part in being able to pursue their interests effectively within it. In doing so, they not only mobilize material capital (to purchase islands, custom avatars and buildings, and the like) but also seek to apply their competencies (in marketing, fundraising, etc.) to this new space. What is more, the brand name that such organizations adopt as the last name for their workers in Second Life stands as a credential.

Credentials (Institutionalized)

Institutionalized cultural capital appears when capacities are formalized into offices and licenses, when an institution with a purview over a certain arena gives its imprimatur to an individual or group as authorized to carry out certain kinds of activities. Thus it is capacity removed from the body of an individual and reified as a credential, and a credentialed individual may or may not have all the competencies thereby implied. The credential nonetheless acts as a resource for action in any case, as a credentialed actor can carry out acts formally allowed by the institution, many of which may in fact be disallowed otherwise. Marrying a couple, firing someone, and speaking or signing a contract on behalf of an institution are instances of the application of institutionalized cultural capital. Bourdieu, speaking specifically of institutionalized cultural capital in the form of academic credentials, elaborates (1986: 248):

> With the academic qualification, a certificate of cultural competence which confers on its holder a conventional, constant, legally guaranteed value with respect to culture, social alchemy produces a form of cultural capital which has a relative autonomy vis-à-vis its bearer and even vis-à-vis the cultural capital he effectively possesses at a given moment in time.

So where do we find credentials in virtual worlds that are not simply imported into the space, as are the brand-based last names noted above? Future research may find it important to look at the rise of education in virtual worlds, both on the part of existing educational institutions (such as the growing community of academics from conventional universities making use of Second Life in their classes) and of new ones (new groups of educators that emerge within and across virtual worlds).

But credentials appear in noneducational contexts in Second Life as well, as the case of Zarf Vantongerloo in Second Life illustrates. Zarf set up shop in Second Life as a notary public, verifying that documents submitted to him are signed by the parties involved at a specific time and retaining a verifiably unchanged version of the document at an offsite (out of Second Life) server.[7] How are his credentials as a notary (he is not one beyond Second Life) established? In his interview with Zarf, Wagner James Au asks:

> "So really . . . the only possible flaw in all this is whether everyone trusts *you* and your code, right?"
>
> ". . . which is true of any notary," Zarf replies. "In real life, the state makes you take a test and you [do] some reporting requirements— but you have to trust that the notary down the street isn't faking your signatures on things. So yes, you have to trust me to not create fake notarizations." He says his code is open source and verifiable in common software packages like OpenSSL, so "the only part of my code you need to trust is how I ensure that my communications are tamper proof."

Here Zarf points to open source verification software to establish his credentials, an innovative way to appeal to credibility in waters that are currently uncharted by any state institution (as Zarf notes elsewhere, his research suggested that in fact virtual notaries might be disallowed by much existing legislation). As academics interested in virtual worlds have suggested (Crawford 2005), following a legal realist approach, there are good grounds for believing that acts such as those by Zarf may generate legitimacy for themselves from the ground up, once they are employed and relied on by sufficient numbers of actors. Public policy might allow new formal laws (or interpretations of existing laws) to follow a then-established cultural practice.

Artifacts (Objectified)

Artifacts are objects that draw a significant amount of their value from their status as repositories of cultural capital. Invested within them are meanings from a given context. Examples include antiques, art, baseball cards, and books. I have noted some of the features of artifacts above in their connection with the market economy, but I want to reintroduce a discussion of an item that I first examined in a previous work (Malaby 2006a): the trading card for Kermitt Quirk's Tringo.

In February 2005 an individual by the name of Kermitt Quirk signed a contract licensing the use of a popular game that he had made, called Tringo, to a company interested in distributing the game worldwide. He designed, scripted, built, and initially distributed the game in Second Life. In Tringo, participants sit facing a large gameboard that displays a number of Tetris-like objects. One at a time, one of these objects is selected and displayed. Each player has a card with a five by five grid and must place the displayed object somewhere on his or her grid. The object is to make complete squares, which give a certain value (the larger the square, the higher the score) and then vanish from the grid. Tringo had already become all the rage in Second Life in late 2004, with residents flocking to Tringo locations to play and socialize, and Quirk turned this popularity into a significant monetary gain.

Linden Lab's marketing team created a remarkable cultural artifact in response to this phenomenon: a trading card. The cards (there were others in a series) were distributed at a variety of events where Linden Lab had a presence in 2005, including academic conferences, trade shows, and the like. Linden Lab aspired to leverage the power of trading cards—which ideally travel through social networks—to generate interest in Second Life and ultimately more users. "Kermitt Quirk's Tringo" is the first card in the "Games" series, and features a screenshot of a game of Tringo (taken within Second Life) on its front, along with the Second Life logo (see figure 2). This is a dense cultural document, filled with carefully written texts that aspire to teach the reader about many things. It seeks to connect things of value (such as income/net worth, connections, occupation) across two different domains of

Figure 2. Kermitt Quirk's Tringo, as presented by Linden Lab in the trading cards they produced for marketing purposes in 2005. The back of the card constitutes an education in Second Life's possibilities.

human action: Second Life and "First Life" (a resident's existence beyond Second Life, in most cases taken to mean "real life," outside online worlds altogether). Also, as a trading card, this object constitutes in itself an artifact that aspires to be valued, and this value furthermore depends on the card's potential for circulation in social networks or material reward through auction.

The card juxtaposes key components of an effort to establish Second Life as an environment with real consequences, material and otherwise, and to do so it points to the various forms of value that actions in Second Life generate. I indicate just a few of these here. Most nota-

Figure 2. (*continued*)

bly, the first item in the trading card's list of Tringo's attributes (analogous to facts about an athlete) is "Creator," which answers one question about the card's purported subject, Tringo. But every item thereafter refers not to Tringo but instead to Kermitt Quirk, who has taken over as the focus of the card's information. We then learn, in quick succession, that he has been a resident since September 4, 2004 (seniority is one of the primary credentials by which social difference is constructed in Second Life), that his First Life occupation is systems analyst/programmer, and that his Second Life occupation is game developer. This juxtaposition places an occupation in Second Life ontologically on a par with one's occupation in the conventional sense.

We learn the name of his business and when it will appear, but it is not a "Second Life Business"—the business as an entity transcends whatever boundary we might expect between First and Second Lives. We are given the location of one of his stores, but the (for the uninitiated) cryptic coordinates are the only indication that this is within Second Life. Lastly, we learn about his net worth, in L$ and US$—again with an element, "L$"—tantalizingly undefined. We then hear of the "business milestone" of Quirk selling distribution rights to Donnerwood Media for "five figures" and hear Quirk himself comment on this, first in brief, and then at length. He points to how the speed of events surprised him, even though he always intended to sell Tringo, and to how he relied on word of mouth to grow his business.

The Tringo trading card, in teaching us about Kermitt Quirk, makes a set of claims about how we are to understand the relationships among a product, money, credentials, skills, and networks. Quirk has credentials outside Second Life (systems analyst/programmer) that can be applied within Second Life. He now has a credential in Second Life, authorized by the signing of the contract with Donnerwood Media, that could be applied beyond it. He has assets, in the form of a business and in-world net worth, the latter of which is readily describable in and, it suggests, convertible into, U.S. dollars. Quirk also has a network of people who know about, enjoy, and recommend his product, such that he as yet does not need to advertise. Beyond this, he, or the game, has a trading card! Again, the card itself aspires to add to the economy of practices by existing in a form distributed by Linden Lab and, potentially, to be valued. More fundamentally, however, Second Life itself is in this picture as an environment where all this can be done, as a place where one can viably leverage skill into connections into credentials into a product into money, and the combinations thereof. But Quirk's success stands in sharp contrast to a contemporary failure, another attempt to make a game in Second Life called Chinatown that was supported and extensively hyped by Linden Lab itself. The success of Tringo, like other such social successes, can seem self-evident, even inevitable, after the fact. The key to understanding the role of failure in Second Life is to realize that such retrospective imposition of meaning always runs the risk of obscuring the contingencies that Second Life's makers face going forward.

New Business

The stakes of Second Life are generated out of the actions of hundreds of thousands of people expending effort in a space where the consequences of their actions can accumulate. That some of these actions can fail, and some succeed, is what gives them meaning. Furthermore, to think in these terms makes it possible for researchers and others to engage seriously the relationships not only within virtual worlds but *among* the various domains of human activity, broadly speaking. The boundaries that only appeared to separate the real and the virtual are fading fast, from both sides, and it is the social actors on the ground who are making use, in every new moment, with every new challenge, of the increased scope that these new domains afford. Without the proper tools to describe their efforts, academic understanding of the digital society will lag irredeemably behind.

For Linden Lab, this entire economy (again, in the broad sense) was what the staff sought to maintain. They strove to protect it from disruption, but equally important (and more a day to day focus of their work) was the continual provision of new affordances, new possibilities for their users, whether in response to user demands or (more often) simply rough guesses about new features that might be useful. For Linden Lab, this was the continual project of providing tools.

2_TOOLS OF THE GODS

It is Friday lunchtime at Linden Lab in mid-2005, and everyone is filing into the kitchen area to partake of the company-provided weekly lunch, an occasion frequently cited by Lindens as a key site for generating company solidarity. This sense of belonging is accomplished, they acknowledge, not only through the act of eating together but also through the shared experience of viewing demos of "secret projects," hearing addresses from Philip Rosedale, and similar, somewhat ritualized activities (for example, new employees may be asked to take a taste from a jar of very, very spicy hot sauce known as "The Man"). As people queue for today's repast (assorted deli sandwiches), I am in the middle of a conversation with another member of the QA (quality assurance) team (not the fashion maven) about the vagaries of academic publishing and my own at the time somewhat pessimistic view of the prospects for publishing ethnographic work on technological production. "Fuck 'em," says a passing Linden, in his inimitable style of utterance, one that combines non-negotiable assertion with a challenge to his listeners to inquire further. "What's that?" I ask, smiling. "Fuck 'em," he reiterates, and continues by concisely condemning the long-established system of academic publishing to the dustbin of history.

They're dinosaurs, he says, and he tells me simply to publish the work myself, on the Web. If it is worthy work, he suggests, it will have an impact. His point made, he moves on.

This brief exchange points to a prevailing—though by no means unanimous—and politically charged disposition toward technology, creativity, individuality, and control that I encountered frequently around Linden Lab. Here I was offered a clear way to proceed in my own situation: via the tools for online publishing available (ostensibly) to all, I could take control of my work and its dissemination without any assistance from an institution. The value of that work would be determined by its reception in a world imagined as a level playing field populated by other individuals pursuing their enlightened self-interest.

Given a moment's pause, we might find it just a bit odd that someone working for an institution that wields an enormous amount of brute technical control over a space with thousands of users would so readily dismiss the contribution of institutions. But this sentiment was by no means uncommon around Linden Lab (although its delivery here was unmistakably individual). To sort out the foundations of this point of view we must delve into the historical and political context of Second Life's creation; that is, how Linden Lab was itself politically situated, and how this manifested itself in its work practice as Lindens went about building, maintaining, and expanding these new domains for a digital society.

(-: :-)

While there is a modernist tendency to characterize new (and not-so-new) technologies as isolated from politics—as value-neutral—scholarship (including a number of excellent contributions from journalists) has made clear that some of the most important developments in computing and networking technology in the United States were inextricably linked to political and more broadly ideological interests. Works by journalists (Kidder 1981, Hiltzik 2000, Waldrop 2001, Markoff 2005) and, more recently, academics (Thomas 2003, Turner

2006) are helpful in filling out the historico-cultural landscape from which computers emerged, particularly in the San Francisco Bay area. Specifically, these works reveal how the development of these technologies and their makers' aspirations for them were inextricably linked to general attitudes about authority that characterized the postwar period in the United States. Important work on the current open source software movement has revealed how its members are the contemporary inheritors of these ideas (Coleman 2004, Kelty 2005). Their strong assertion of software as a form of free speech "underscores ideas of individual autonomy, self-development, and a value-free marketplace for the expression of ideas" (Coleman 2004: 510), while stridently denying any specific political claims in what Coleman calls a "political agnosticism" (509).

A common theme of these works is a remarkable and mutually confirming combination of a deeply held skepticism toward "top-down" decision making—with a corresponding resistance to (and even resentment of) the institutional control of technology—and a deep faith in the ability of technology to provide solutions when made widely available. The contrast here is with computing as it existed in institutions through the 1960s: mainframe computing demanded specialized and controlled access to the most powerful tool in an institution, and its enduring image is that of the mainframe in the glass room, accessible only to a priesthood of those empowered to tend it.

The attitude that arose in reaction to this image, these books suggest, reflects the antiestablishment politics of the period and found purchase in the distinctive disposition of engineers toward new technologies, corporate organizations, and a particular version of liberalism. This disposition was strongly situated in the actual practice of programming (as compared to discursive argumentation; see Kelty 2005). One can find in these works multiple versions of what seems the same story of how this disposition was born for individuals—it is the recurring theme of young programmer after programmer, given access to off-hours mainframe usage in universities and other institutionalized settings, coming away with a passionate commitment to the wide-ranging potential of computing and networking technology, but a potential for them better realized when placed into the hands of creative individuals not beholden to institutional demands (see, for example, Kidder 1981: 95). As Coleman writes (2004: 511–512):

> Programmers over decades of intense interaction come to viscerally experience the computer as a general purpose machine that can be infinitely programmed to achieve any task through the medium of software written by humans with a computer language. The technological potential for unlimited programmable capabilities melds with what is seen as the expansive ability for programmers to create. For programmers, computing in a dual sense, as a technology and as an activity, becomes a total realm for the freedom of creation and expression.

The issue of creation and engineering is central to Linden Lab's project in particular, as the making *of* the world of Second Life stands in a strange and mutually constructive relationship to the making *in* the world on the part of its users.

To understand how this approach to authority and technology characterizes high-tech companies like Linden Lab, we might begin by keeping in mind an underemphasized but important connection between national interests and technological development in the United States (see Downey 1998). While the military roots of the Internet are well-known, the oft-cited way in which the architecture of the Internet was designed to route around disruptions caused by (nuclear) attacks is not often linked, as it should be, to a broader set of ideas about systems, control, and collaboration that developed in postwar (cold war) America. To accomplish that in brief here, I rely on the books above, but most heavily on Fred Turner's work on Stewart Brand and the *Whole Earth Catalog* (2006), because it is Brand's language of tools that continued to echo most loudly around the desks of Linden Lab in 2005. The broader issue that Turner confronts is the rise of collaborative work on technology and how it fit with a set of ideas about authority and the imagined properties of systems, and all this constitutes a helpful background to understanding, above all, what "tools" were around

Linden Lab. Once we make these connections, the pithy relegation of traditional systems of control (like academic publishing) to the trash heap make sense as part of a larger (and ultimately modernist and optimistic) stance toward the future and the role of technology in it (a technoliberalism) that was prevalent around Linden Lab.

Rigging History

Before we embark on forging that connection, a bit more must be said about Linden Lab and its early history. Seeking to take advantage of the general familiarity with technology around Linden Lab to help me understand its past, I initiated a wiki project (that is, a collectively edited text-based Web page), in partnership with Wagner James Au, a journalist writing about Second Life as a contractor for Linden Lab at the time. We set up a Web page with some text inviting Lindens to record their memories of events in Linden Lab's or Second Life's history that were significant in some way, whether personally (such as accounts of people's first days at Linden Lab, or first encounters with Second Life) or organizationally (such as the official launch of Second Life in June 2003). We intended this project primarily to be a space for Lindens to share with each other their imagined history of their project, and we did not seek to maintain any control over the site after letting them know about it and our plans to quote from it in our work. At the end of 2005 I took a snapshot of the Linden Lab History Wiki (that is, I saved a version current to December 5 of that year), and I rely on it here to supplement information from interviews as well as other sources (such as blogs) and introduce one account of the beginnings of Linden Lab. I return to different moments in Linden Lab's past at later points in the book.

Philip Rosedale contributed first to the wiki, and his earliest entries are dated 1992–1996. Here we can get a sense of his early interests (as a student at the University of California—San Diego) that later led him to found Linden Lab. At that time he imagined, and began working on, a full-body virtual reality interface (later known as "the Rig"—it was kept, in pieces, in one of the rooms at Linden Lab) that a person would be "strapped into" and through which they could act, with the full range of gross to fine motor movements, inside a virtual environment that he planned to build. He abandoned quite early the idea of making its many parts actually move (the way a mouse moves to move a cursor on a computer screen) but hit upon the idea of pressure-sensitive contacts that could lead one to "move" in a virtual environment without actually moving significantly offline. In a lengthy interview as well as other conversations with me, Rosedale pointed to science fiction and the work of Neal Stephenson (specifically, his novel *Snow Crash*, 1992) as providing the inspiration for this virtual environment. Stephenson's term for it, *metaverse*, was the term Lindens used most frequently when reaching for a literary label for Second Life.[1]

In 1996 the project was put on hold. As Rosedale put it in the wiki, "in 1995 . . . [I] got sidetracked into the interesting problem of making compressed live video work over a modem. Ended up selling my video technology and myself to RealNetworks in early '96 and fell into the dreamless sleep of a hyperaccelerated startup for the next three and a half years." Rosedale ended up as chief technology officer at RealNetworks, and he quit in 1999 (a good time to leave a dotcom boom company), after which he immediately laid the groundwork to found what would become Linden Lab. He found a space to start the company (a "garage" on Linden Street in San Francisco), and at this point the focus of development shifted somewhat to the software architecture of the virtual world itself. The expertise in streaming media technologies was helpful, he told me, for working through these ideas. Soon he began hiring people to help him, and the world began to take shape. In addition to his own investment, Mitch Kapor (founder of Lotus Development) later invested in the company (in 2001). Work culminated in a demonstration of (then-named) "Lindenworld" at DEMO 2002 (a conference focused on hands-on demonstrations of new technologies). Following this, the company began to hire more employees, until their formal launch of Second Life in June 2003.

In considering this early history, a number of things stand out, and I can highlight only a few of them briefly here. In Rosedale's initial idea for what became Second Life he did not anticipate how the space would become a social space. I asked in our interview whether they thought they were building a society in the first years of the company. As he put it:

> Given my background there was always a tendency to focus a little bit on the technical because I found the technical problems to be so fascinating involved with creating this. But I think as a person who had a lot of passion for the idea, I was always struck by the expressive and not so much societal elements, although I have to say: I think that a lot of the enthusiasm that I have now for the kind of social change or societal change that might result from something like Second Life getting global, or getting a lot bigger—to where it matters. . . . I think a lot of that stuff I kind of came to understand more as we went along. I didn't go in feeling like we're going to make people's lives better. But I did go into it feeling like none of it was interesting unless there were a lot of people involved.
>
> . . .
>
> I think that it was more emergent as we saw things start to happen and we saw people be affected by Second Life. It was then that we said, "Well, you know, it might be that an environment that has this really, sort of, super-enhanced projective, creative element to it could actually be a kind of a bandwidth-increasing thing between people in general." And then we started writing—I can't remember, maybe in 2003, or 2004—started writing about—and Cory [Ondrejka] as well—about how if you grossly, if you just increase the communicative bandwidth between individuals that there's almost no arguing, unless you're really taking a contrarian position, you know, that that probably makes them better. . . . The whole sort of combination of creative self-expression and the transparent society.

What is striking here, and instructive, is the emphasis on individuals not, initially at least, as social beings but as individual creators who would in Second Life create together, seemingly without Linden Lab imagining the possibility of the development of broader social effects.

This is consistent with the approach of the New Communalists as Turner describes them, given the similar emphasis on groups (of *Whole Earth Catalog* readers, of members of communes) as accumulations of individuals, each pursuing an enlightened self-interest. The idea, as Rosedale described it, was for people to create "experiences" for other users, and that experiences that were popular would persist: "[I was] into selection pressure and evolutionary emergence as the prime movers in this."

The commitment to shared experience was reflected in Second Life's code. Every time a resident acts in Second Life, whether doing something as common and simple as engaging in text-based chat or changing clothes or appearance, but most obviously and grandly when scripting or building, the resident's activity is represented in gestures and actions of the avatar itself, visible to any nearby Second Life users. What is more, if an object is being worked on, the changes to that object are observable by others in the world in real time, even down to click-to-click changes in, say, the object's color as the user tries different points on the building tool's color wheel. When I discovered that wrapping a Spanish tile texture onto my tower's dome stretched a single tile around it and created an entirely new look, this was the result of such a real time change applied to my object (the dome) as I tried different textures in my inventory. And when I did so, any user nearby could have seen it. This publicly visible creation was an intentional decision by the developers of Second Life, and, according to one developer, it ran counter to a number of users' preferences. It was, however, consistent with, as he put it, the promotion of "shared experience," the idea that while in world users would be able to be in touch with what others were doing, and he described it as a way to combat the "balkanization of thought." The social in Second Life, we can note, was highly individualist. It rested on the idea that the only social exchange that would occur there was an exchange of ideas, of expression through technological creation (Kelty 2005, Coleman 2004).

Because of this preconception, one gets the sense that Rosedale was to a certain extent brought up short by the development in Second Life of communities that saw themselves as such, which recognized and celebrated distinctive identities and sought to include or exclude not as individual actors but as participants in socio-political struggles. Rosedale cited the increasing involvement of early employees from gaming backgrounds (including later vice presidents Robin Harper and Cory Ondrejka) as important for making the adjustment to this dimension of what Second Life was becoming. They provided the "behavioral psychology" component that Linden Lab needed. When I asked him to expand on that point, he said the employees helped them think in "game theoretic terms. . . . What do you want to motivate people to do? What are the rewards?"

But despite the increasing need to recognize their own inevitable role in governance, the core aspect of the relationship between Linden Lab and Second Life users did not change: Linden Lab provided the tools, and the world, and the users would *make* things. If, initially, their creations were imagined only as things for other users to encounter and experience (an interactive house meant to simulate a schizophrenic episode; a recreation of a 1950s roadside gas station, complete with vintage Coke machine; a working Ferris wheel), the recognition that users would also be involved in other kinds of making (of alliances, of relationships, of community) still, for Linden Lab, called for the provision of tools.

Legitimate Tools

> We are as gods and might as well get good at it. So far, remotely done power and glory—as via government, big business, formal education, church—has succeeded to the point where gross defects obscure actual gains. In response to this dilemma and to these gains a realm of intimate, personal power is developing—power of the individual to conduct his own education, find his own inspiration, shape his own environment, and share his adventure with whoever is interested. Tools that aid this process are sought and promoted by the *Whole Earth Catalog*.
>
> —Inside cover statement of every edition of the *Whole Earth Catalog* (Brand 1969)

The counterculture of 1960s America included an important segment of thinkers that embraced technology as part of their picture of how American (in fact, human) life would be transformed as existing institutions collapsed. To read some of the statements of the important figures of the time, in particular those of Stewart Brand, the founder of the *Whole Earth Catalog*, is to be transported to a time in which the possibilities of technology, wedded to a particular conception of how to organize human activity, promised nothing less than a utopian future.

In this promise, "tools" was a key word. The first issue of the catalog had, above a photograph of the entire earth (taken during a 1967 NASA expedition), the title *Whole Earth Catalog / access to tools* (see Turner 2006: 79). Above the statement of purpose quoted above, there was a statement of the catalog's function that helps to give further shape to what was meant by this term (Brand 1969):

> The WHOLE EARTH CATALOG functions as an evaluation and access device. With it, the user should know better what is worth getting and where and how to do the getting.
> An item is listed in the CATALOG if it is deemed:
>
> 1. Useful as a tool,
> 2. Relevant to independent education,
> 3. High quality or low cost,
> 4. Not already common knowledge,
> 5. Easily available by mail.
>
> This information is continually revised according to the experience and suggestions of CATALOG users and staff.

Turner writes that "a complex series of attitudes toward technology were embedded . . . within both the statement and the pages of the *Catalog*" (2006: 91), and he goes on to highlight several themes in an illuminating discussion. For our purposes one of the important themes is the focus on the *individual* (the "user"), who is someone cast as pursuing an independent education. As such, the catalog is a device of *evaluation* for that user. The question of whether the catalog is the product of (prior) evaluation or provided so the user can make evaluations is neatly elided by the last line, which testifies to the continual revision of the catalog "according to the experience and suggestions of

CATALOG users and staff." Here already is a presaging of the position of continual revision that is put forth around Linden Lab as characterizing the company's relationship to Second Life and its users. This again connects to what tools are: a tool is something that has a use, but this use need not be imagined as predetermined. The creative component in this account of the individual and technology is to be found in the application of tools in new ways, generating new practices and outcomes.

Another strand of this thought has a direct bearing on what I found around Linden Lab: emergent properties and how legitimate they are as a basis for self-governance. Well before Stewart Brand, according to Turner, and in an ironic contrast to the antiestablishment feeling to come, a new style of work practice emerged in the context of World War II and the cold war, with that era's constant demands on the United States to innovate in a number of areas (the atomic bomb being the most famous example). In places like MIT's Radiation Lab, members of the military, industry, and academia had to find a way to work together even though no single vertical institution governed them. The successes produced by such collaborations resonated with ideas put forth by some of their members. Norbert Wiener and Julian Bigelow, through war-related research on systematizing antiaircraft weaponry, had begun to apply the metaphor of computing on a grand scale to humans and their society. As Turner writes, "Wiener and Bigelow offered up a picture of humans and machines as dynamic, collaborating elements in a single, highly fluid, socio-technical system. Within that system, control emerged not from the mind of a commanding officer but from the complex, probabilistic interactions of humans, machines, and events around them" (2006: 21).

For an understanding of Linden Lab, the most important effect of the rise of this thinking about socio-technical systems and controls was the implicit legitimacy that such effects seemed to have. The suggestion (which can be traced back to Adam Smith's "invisible hand") is that the emergent properties of complex interactions enjoy a certain degree of rightness just by virtue of being emergent. Like the market in the imagination of many in the capitalist era, these effects are examples of self-governance, imagined to occur in something like "natural" or unconstrained conditions. Therefore they provide an appealing alternative to top-down logics of legitimate authority. Around Linden Lab, these ideas about technology as a tool and emergent properties as legitimate self-governance circulated not only in the appeal to "tools" but in a number of other ways. One could note the circulation of texts around Linden Lab that supported this way of thinking about work, such as two books whose grand titles are worth quoting in full: Thomas Malone's *The Future of Work: How the New Order of Business Will Shape Your Organization, Your Management Style, and Your Life* (2004), and James Surowiecki's *The Wisdom of Crowds: Why the Many are Smarter than the Few and How Collective Wisdom Shapes Business, Economies, Societies, and Nations* (2004).[2]

These ideas about authority and technology were held by Lindens as applying both to Linden Lab's creation, Second Life, and to themselves as an organization. In that sense, it may be better to characterize them as *ideals*; their status as the right way to go about doing things was, at least for many at the company, unassailable. The most explicit statement of these ideals, as they applied to Linden Lab itself, is to be found in the "Tao of Linden," a company document that is also publicly available from Linden Lab's Web site, and which is worth reading in light of the New Communalist ideals charted out above (it is reprinted in full in appendix A). Given the way in which its ideals were held to apply both to Second Life and to Linden Lab, it is not a surprise to find that in certain ways this attitude toward tools was also inscribed into the very technologies by which the employees attempted to organize their work practice.

The near-ubiquitous appeal to "tools" around Linden Lab throughout 2005 ("We need to provide tools for our users to solve this problem"; "The island management tools are broken") is consistent with a deep commitment to and acknowledgment of Second Life as a domain for empowered users to create content with a minimum of vertical direction or control. Just like the users of the *Whole Earth Catalog*, Second Life users are given *access* to tools, and this issue of access (often glossed as "open participation" around Linden Lab) was of continuing importance. In "The Mission of Linden Lab" (reprinted herein as appendix B), a November 2006 Web log post, Philip Rosedale wrote:

> We will not move in a direction that will restrict Second Life as to the number of people it can conceivably reach. This means that we will struggle to have Second Life work in any country, be available to anyone wanting to use it, and work well on a wide range of computing devices. As another example, we will not restrict Second Life by adding constraints which might make it more compelling to a specific subset of people but have the effect of reducing the broadest capabilities it offers to everyone for communication and expression.

Broad, theoretically universal participation was essential to the ideals of Second Life, as Linden Lab saw them. But how universal could a bounded and contrived online world be? This is a complex question. When many of the New Communalists sought in the latter part of the 1960s to make their own, set-apart communes within which to pursue these ideals, they could be seen as attempting to create the first virtual worlds, at least in the sense of a contrived and self-contained environment. But they ran into serious difficulties, with the vast majority of the communes collapsing. Stewart Brand ultimately decried self-sufficiency as an ideal in 1975 and soon after turned to the ideas of Gregory Bateson, for whom only a wide-open (that is, world-level) vision of connected information could promote the systemwide effects the movement saw as the holy grail of self-governance (Turner 2006: 118–125).

Second Life, it seems, squares this circle, being both an entirely synthetic creation and at least arguably universally accessible. While the effort to make a world has clear resonances with the attempts to make New Communalists' communes, the issues of self-sufficiency and access are somewhat elided. Linden Lab could appeal to the putatively wide-open Internet, as well as to the attempt to connect Second Life's economy to conventional economies (the product of the revamping of Second Life in late 2003), as ways in which Second Life was not making the communes' mistake. But a core paradox remained. While

Stewart Brand and his staff could put the whole earth on the cover of their publication and play a large role in setting the terms by which a generation came to see technology as a personal tool, they were not in a position to change that planet's physics with a few well-placed edits to a line of code. Even the communes were imperfectly governable, constrained by the familiar limits of offline authority.

Second Life, by contrast, holds out the promise of wide-open access and broadly distributed tools through the personal computers that its users have. The personal computer was heralded as a particularly flexible tool that put power in the hands of individual users, and Turner's account is amplified by the other parts of the story told by Michael Hiltzik (2000), M. Mitchell Waldrop (2001), John Markoff (2005) and Tracy Kidder (1981). But even though its users encounter it through their personal computers, Linden Lab can never escape the special authority it wields over Second Life, in particular the degree to which its architectural decisions shape human action in the environment, perhaps more deeply than any other factor in play. The paradox for Linden Lab is how to reconcile the contradiction between the company's position as the entity that provides the tools and its position as the entity that provides the world in which those tools are used. In Tom Boellstorff's (2008) powerful portrayal of how Second Life users come to see the crafting of themselves as an available and intentional project, to be achieved through making rather than knowing (*techne* rather than *episteme*), he shows how successful Linden Lab has been at putting forth an ideal of agency for its users that accords with this technoliberal promise. For their part, however, this provision of tools leads to a certain amount of ambivalence.

In an interview with one of the developers at Linden Lab, I asked about the trend in online games (Neverwinter Nights, among others) of providing to the users some of the same tools that the developers use to make things in the world. (This question was prompted by my observation that in Second Life the basic content-creation tools—building, scripting, and texture mapping—are the same ones that game content makers have for computer games in general.) The developer began to talk about just what it meant to provide tools to users, and he highlighted the importance of carefully *limiting* what those tools could do: "Most game developers don't ever release all of their tools because so many of them are just one-offs that they do really quickly . . . and therefore have a lot of holes in them in terms of the user perspective [and] can be dangerous." The provision of tools by Linden Lab to its users shows how different the process of their selection is from that claimed by the *Whole Earth Catalog*. The divide between those with access to what is under the hood and those who must not have this access shaped both the set and the form of the tools in Second Life.

This social distinction also held true for the tools Lindens relied on as a company, for not everyone at Linden Lab was awash in code, able to remake the technological parameters of their work as needed. Many Lindens used tools in their daily work that had been created by other Lindens—specifically, developers. Software-based tools moved around Linden Lab, but they traveled in one direction: from developers to people in other areas ("What tools do we need to improve or create to make our land sales process better?"; "We're still waiting for a new CSR tool"). This highlights the fundamental divide that shaped tensions within the company—that between the "devs" (developers; i.e., programmers) and, well, everyone else. An emerging tension appeared around Linden Lab between the tool users and the tool creators, as it were. The question of who were the gods (in the words of the *Whole Earth Catalog*) and who were not rumbled quietly along like a distant runaway locomotive.

As Second Life grew in size and complexity, so did Linden Lab. The pressure to acknowledge and perhaps amplify vertical control increased, but with some segments feeling more pressure than others. This tension became the preoccupying focus of the employees' organizational lives. For those who felt technology provided the means for individuals creatively to express themselves and pursue their own interests (and thereby serve an emergent good), this preoccupation with the dangers of vertical authority was the result of the same politically charged disposition, one that tended to treat top-down or vertical decision making as the antithesis of empowered and creative action. As people at Linden Lab witnessed their creation and their company growing, this fear of a loss of liberty reached, at times, a fever pitch. In what remains of this chapter, I illustrate how this tension between political ideals *around* Linden Lab and the political positioning *of* Linden Lab played out in work practice, and in particular how a turn to software development and design frequently sought *practically* to resolve a difficulty that could not be answered *discursively*.

Horizontal Hold

One remarkable feature of how work got done at Linden Lab during the time of my research was the way struggles over ongoing decision making took practical turns, as one participant or another within a given project sought to move the decision forward not through more conversation or debate but through the display of practical expertise. This was most commonly a move of the developers within Linden Lab, any one of whom might have been seen to drop everything and code (that is, write one or more computer programs or parts of programs) for a matter of hours or days until he or she unveiled the work to other members of the team or even perhaps the company as a whole—at a Friday lunch, for example.

One such incident occurred early in 2005, when I noticed that a number of Lindens were away from their desks at the same time. Asking another Linden nearby the reason, I was told that there was a meeting on a lighting/shading effects feature to be added into Second Life, an issue that I had learned had posed some significant technical challenges. Later that afternoon, a group of about four to five (later, six to eight) Lindens suddenly formed around one developer's desk—he had taken some ideas from the meeting and combined them with some of his own and quickly mocked up a lighting/shading demo that he demonstrated, seated, to others as they stood in a tight semicircle behind him. I headed over to get a glimpse as well and saw him manipulating his mouse to rotate a directional light around a complex textured object on his monitor.

This kind of event was common within Linden Lab and was closely tied to the phrase "proof of concept," one that merits some critical attention, as it reveals a bit more of the picture of the relationship of programming practice to such weighty concepts as truth and verification; that is, how practice often provided an answer to questions about what could be done under what conditions (technical and other constraints). When someone at Linden in 2005 claimed to have created, or to have been planning to create, a proof of concept, this was a reliable sign that a difference of opinion had arisen among members of a team working together on a project or between individual employees and their immediate superiors. But to understand the nature of this kind of disagreement, and why it can pose an organizational challenge for Linden Lab, one must first understand the overall management structure of Linden Lab at the time of my research.

On the surface, Linden Lab strove to have an organizational structure that resisted vertical authority to the point of denying its existence almost entirely, for the reasons already mentioned. The layout of the company's work space reflected this. At its Second Street location, which it occupied until mid-April 2005, all employees were in one room, each with a desk that was part of a cluster of three or four such desks, each of which faced the center. There were no cubicles or other walls (Rosedale: "Never. Death first."), and thus the workspace allowed quite open sight lines to all employees, and the top-level Lindens were in the room like everyone else (Rosedale's desk was at a cluster with a developer and a content creator). This approach carried over to Linden Lab's new space, on Sansome Street, which boasted a much larger central room (made even larger by knocking down a wall) to accommodate the increasing numbers of employees.

I quickly noticed several practices that fit this organization of space, such as the proof of concept demo. Given the ways that technology circulated information about what others were doing in the company, one could observe the corollary that Lindens would raise their heads and scan the room to see if someone they might want to talk to was available (perhaps passing through on the way back from the kitchen). Then the person might stand up and make his or her way over to the

Linden's desk, arriving at the same time for a discussion. Thus a careful, learned habit had emerged to fit the open work space and manage one's interruptions of others. One could go further and notice the difference between a visiting Linden standing at a desk talking to its occupant, without leaning over (likely to be a brief meeting), a visitor kneeling down to talk at the desk (signaling a longer and perhaps more private conversation), and the visitor looking around to grab one of the many extra chairs or stools that were scattered about the room and sitting in it for an extensive chat. Groupings of two with at least one person standing were clearly considered public, and others (passing or nearby) would look to hear what was being talked about and perhaps walk over to join. The lighting demo was further distinct as an example of a meeting type. Here the desk owner is oriented toward his or her own computer screen, running a demo, while an audience forms behind. These gatherings were likely to bring other Lindens over to take a look at the screen. In these ways, the horizontal circulation of information and bodies had a marked effect on Linden Lab and was reflected in the employees' organization of space.

Even so, vertical decision making played an enormous role within Linden Lab, as it does in every organization. In some respects, what I found was almost a perfect reversal of what Kidder discovered in one department of the company he studied in *Soul of a New Machine* (1981). Where Kidder found disorder masquerading as order (1981: 120), I saw in Linden Lab order beneath a claim to disorder. Rosedale, Robin Harper (vice president of marketing, then of community), and Cory Ondrejka (vice president of product development) exerted a great deal of influence over the people who worked around Linden Lab (they were joined later in 2005 by a new vice president of marketing and a general counsel); their judgments and preferences were as, if not more, important for whether any given initiative was pursued than was horizontal collaboration. For some directors, the Lindens that worked in their areas tended to be clustered near them. Despite the frequently heard assertion at the time that Linden Lab "doesn't have" departments, departments did exist, organizing, among other things, compensation. Each group had an identifiable leader. They were the bosses to whom people reported. (A listing of the departments at Linden Lab at this time would include: development [production], quality assurance [QA], system administration [sysadmin], marketing, content, community, finance, administration, and customer service.) As was frequently noted with some levity, Ondrejka was always in the darkest corner, surrounded by "devs" (many developers prefer a low light level to avoid glare on their computer screens, on which they manage many lines of code at a time). But this arrangement was not entirely due to a preference for dark spaces. When Linden Lab began planning to move to the new office, there was some debate about how desk spots would be chosen. Although the system they settled on attempted to give everyone the freedom to negotiate competing desires, seniority was the arbiter of last resort. Since most of the oldest employees were developers, they tended to dictate the spatial distribution of Lindens based on their early choices. (One could say that while the ideals of Linden Lab sought to celebrate one kind of cultural capital, competence, to the exclusion of either connections [social capital] or credentials [title, or seniority], in practice these other forms of capital were alive and well around Linden Lab.)

In any case, and not surprisingly to anyone who has studied organizations, it was the dialectical tension *between* vertical and horizontal kinds of authority that governed work around Linden Lab. Nonetheless, the explicit denial of the role or power of vertical decision making meant that I was likely to hear only of the ways in which the company's direction and decision making flowed from the collective judgment of its employees. This is not to say that employees did not have a significant degree of freedom and opportunity to pursue their own projects (especially developers, as nondevelopers were quick to point out to me) but only to make clear the divergence between the denial of verticality in the employees' overall representation of themselves and the practical combination of these forms for how work got done at the company.[3]

This divergence between representation and practice is sensible in political terms and serves as an index of how important the plausible representation of the company as committed to individual autonomy was for many of its members. Again, as the company and Second Life grew, this tension became more apparent and difficult to deny; the simple act of efficiently sharing information throughout the company demanded structural changes, and it is from a moment in this transition that I draw an illustrative example. It shows not only how the tension above played out as the company grew but also how in crises a turn to technology, and specifically technology that could be further manipulated to create a system, characterized Linden Lab.

(-: :-)

When I first arrived at Linden Lab, I quickly learned of the preeminent tool for distributing information about the many projects going on within the company: "Achievements and Objectives" ("As & Os" for short—at times As were listed as "Accomplishments" on some Lindens' documents). Connected to an established management practice known as "management by objectives," based on the ideas of Peter Drucker (1954), the system of As & Os at Linden Lab had been in place since early 2001 and served several functions (including periodic determinations of compensation by the president and other directors—the dimension of material capital is ever-present). Here I focus on their role in disseminating information horizontally through the company. Every employee, every week, was required to write up an As & Os document which would then be sent to everyone else in the company, and everyone was correspondingly required to read all the other As & Os. Linden Lab had approximately thirty-five employees at the end of 2004, and each of them listed his or her achievements over the past week and outlined his or her objectives—the projects the employee continued to work on.

Linden Lab As & Os had a number of features that are useful to keep in mind through what follows. First, they were text documents, and therefore their layout could be customized to a great degree (while keeping to the convention of a single page). This extended to a certain fungibility about what exactly counted as an achievement or an objective. A partially completed objective would often be listed as an achievement, with a parenthetical note at the end indicating "Not Done" or "Partial" (with completed tasks having a "Done" following their entries). Lindens would at times add a "Bonus" category at the end of their As & Os, listing achievements that were not previously listed as objectives. Here are some examples of lines from various Lindens' As & Os in January and February 2005 (apart from the bullets, the original formatting is preserved, though I have removed identifying details):

As:
- Schedule [applicant] for an interview DONE (actually, [a Linden] wants to wait)
- Modeling [in world content for LL sponsored marketing event] (begun)
- Spec out the details of the Greeter process and create first draft of copy that will appear at each step <done>
- DONE Investigate possible . . . exploit by [user], reported by [a Linden] (I don't think an exploit was used, however I did find one possible exploit which I will be plugging this week)
- Collect forum moderator software options for review—partial

Os:
- Meet with html layout guy, hammer out some details and write wiki page on it
- Follow up on sim lag on private islands
- Model/script moth canoe
- More furniture requests

Bonus:
- 1st draft of GDC party Planning Document (DONE)
- Release meeting for 1.5.14
- Secret web-video editing project for [a Linden]
- Letter of intent on new office signed

Lindens thus each exerted a significant influence on the framing of what they did each week through the flexibility of the As & Os system. There are comments about other Lindens, and their role in the writer's work practice. There are different ways to signal what has been done, partially done, or begun. Bonus items tend to be less clearly As or Os: Is the meeting an achievement? Is the editing project an objective? Related to this is an aspect of As & Os and how they were used that is critically important to recognize for the present discussion: Lindens were free to select the level at which tasks were defined. Thus, very large ("Kick off teen grid development") or open-ended items ("Help [another Linden] get up and running") could still be listed as objectives despite the lack of clear conditions for their completion. At the other end, objectives (and achievements) could be extremely narrow—the subtasks of subtasks of subtasks. No matter how large or small, they get to count in the As & Os as one line like any other.

A second important feature of As & Os is that they were sent from each Linden's e-mail account, and thus they each appeared at a certain time (the bulk of them in the latter part of Monday morning) in everyone's e-mail program. This meant that the simple arrival of an As & Os from a specific Linden could prompt a memory in another Linden, who might be moved to read that one first or otherwise select from As & Os as they arrived (depending on how that Linden set up their e-mail program to notify about incoming mail, etc.)—it might provide the impetus for a Linden to watch for another Linden's free moment and begin an impromptu meeting of the kinds described above.

Given that many projects were accomplished in teams, one of the important effects of this aspect of As & Os was that it not only gave Lindens a sense of the various things going on at any given time across the company but also provided them with an opportunity to get involved in projects in which they were particularly interested, with a clear indication of whom to approach. For Philip Rosedale and others, this generated an important emergent effect on how Linden Lab's decision making got done. They felt that by sharing information that enabled Lindens to identify and then contribute to initiatives they saw as important, the As & Os, in a way consistent with lateral decision making and individual autonomy, generated a form of collective wisdom (they frequently cited the Surowiecki book [2004]) that shaped company priorities. That is, in their view this process was consistent with the libertarian "hacker ethic" (Levy 1984, Thomas

2003). Correspondingly, in their view, it also implicitly generated legitimate (in fact, in Rosedale's view, optimal) business decisions for Linden Lab in the way that people gravitated to tasks that they saw as important or in which they felt invested. This process was frequently pointed to as generating a net effect of optimal collective judgment about setting priorities—such as, for example, whether to focus on fixing bugs or adding features to Second Life. It was also held to account for what Rosedale asserted was an abnormally high level of per capita productivity in the company.

In effect, the As & Os were performing a number of functions for Linden Lab in addition to distributing information laterally within the company and generating patterns of attention that in the view of some employees reflected a "collective wisdom" about what Linden should do next. Individual Lindens regularly remarked to me that the As & Os helped them think about and organize their own work, individually. They were also used by managers to keep track of employee work and to determine compensation. Over the course of 2005, however, Linden Lab more than doubled in size, reaching almost seventy employees by the end of the year. Even when I first arrived, I heard Lindens frequently voice the complaint that there were too many As & Os to keep up without neglecting their other work. With the company straining at the seams in this regard, the issue percolated over the first few months of the year without a clear solution presenting itself.

In February 2005, however, the company had begun using Jira, a Web-based bug and feature-tracking application developed by Atlassian Software Systems of Australia. Jira is designed to help a group of people keep track of the development of a software product and allows for the relatively straightforward coding of further tools that can be layered onto its software to make use of the information it tracks. People involved in a project can see what bugs, issues, and features are being tracked by the program and who is working on those items, subscribe for notifications about changes in them, and add comments, including links to similar or overlapping items.

While the program was designed for software development specifically, Rosedale quickly came to see Jira as a solution to the increasingly cumbersome use of As & Os for information dissemination and collective prioritization. Whereas the As & Os were organized by individuals, Jira was organized by "tasks," and this term seemed flexible enough to accommodate a range of company tasks, including those not directly related to changes in the Second Life software. So, for example, the office manager could create a task in Jira concerning the installation of additional Ethernet infrastructure for the office, or someone involved with marketing could create a task for Linden Lab's efforts at an industry convention. Jira for Rosedale could ideally become a representation of everything people in Linden Lab were doing, to the extent that Lindens created tasks within Jira. This Rosedale heavily encouraged them to do (in an example of the kind of vertical mandate that was rarely acknowledged as such). Unlike the As & Os, Jira's database of tasks could be manipulated via code—Linden Lab was free to write queries, design customized web interfaces, or otherwise subject the "stuff" in Jira to the operations of code. The As & Os, as text documents (often idiosyncratically formatted), were amenable only to word searches and the like; and given the lack of uniformity in how two Lindens might refer even to the same project, querying As & Os in this way was unproductive. Jira offered both more flexibility and more standardization, though the implications of the latter went largely undiscussed.

This is because, as flexible as Jira was, it still could not "see" certain kinds of nondiscrete tasks. These tasks were "ongoing" or "recurring" (as they were called around Linden Lab). Lindens were regularly reminded that ongoing work did not belong in As & Os, although Lindens often managed to make them fit in their weekly sheets anyway. Handling the customer service phone queue (a never-ending job) was one example. Consider the following segment of the "Tao of Linden" (see appendix A):

Make Weekly Progress
We believe that every person should make specific, visible individual contributions that moves [sic] the company forward every week. Projects must be broken down into measurable tasks so that making weekly progress is possible. This is a principle that almost no one

believes is true when they first hear it, yet everyone who keeps to this principle over the course of several months is stunned by the amount of progress made during that time. Set weekly goals and report progress to everyone. Regardless how big what you are working on may be, you can always break it down this way. Give it a try.

Not only were Lindens discouraged from reporting ongoing, never-completed tasks, Jira also missed other kinds of work. It did not make sense, for example, to create Jira tasks for things that demanded immediate, urgent attention, such as the sudden breakdown of one of the servers that ran one of the squares ("sims") of Second Life's "grid." These servers were housed at the co-location, and if a failure could not be handled remotely, then a Linden needed to hightail it to the "colo" and fix the problem. Taking even the few moments necessary to create a Jira task to reflect this struck the system administrators for Linden Lab ("sysadmins") as ludicrous.

"Infrastructural" tasks of this sort (as another Linden labeled them to me) thus tended not to be visible to Jira—in a way that recalls, strikingly, Adam Smith's own insight that transportation infrastructure (road systems, bridges, etc.), as well as education, are essentially invisible to the market. Certain Lindens tried to work around this, typically by setting up a Jira project as an ongoing "task," then making discrete subtasks for specific events that could be completed. One of these was "Trips to the Apple Store" (for servicing Linden Lab's Macs) as an ongoing project, with specific trips entered as subtasks, which could then be completed. But many ongoing tasks could not be finessed into Jira in this way. This has implications for the status of creativity—and jobs that counted as creative jobs around Linden Lab.

In any case, for the problem of disseminating information in the wake of the imminent breakdown of As & Os (which continued to be used for other purposes, increasingly as a matter of individual employee choice), Jira suggested an attractive practical solution. The initial idea was that every Linden would, as they had with As & Os, enter their work tasks into Jira, whether directly related to software development or not. From the Jira main page, anyone in the company could search tasks, group them by Linden (to achieve something similar to the As & Os), or otherwise sort them. Again, the fact that Jira was a piece of customizable software suggested a range of inchoate and powerful possibilities for a number of Lindens. Rosedale was the most prominent and vocal supporter, but support for at least exploring this option was strong among developers (the single largest contingent in the company, which had approximately forty-two employees at this time).

Others from non–software engineering backgrounds were less sanguine about Jira's potential for replacing As & Os in this regard. "Forming a corporate culture around a product—[a] project management tool—that's a new one by me," said a Linden involved in community management (including customer service). His chief concern, and it was shared by others, was whether Jira really added anything to how they already went about getting work done. A key difference, he noted, between As & Os and Jira was the possibility that a task could be entered into Jira by someone other than the person in a position to accomplish it. For As & Os, any entry for such a project necessarily involved the writer as a participant in the project; even "Get [a Linden] to code a new tool for land sales" involves the writer as a participant in moving the project forward. In Jira, however, someone can initiate a project that that person feels needs to be done and name someone (optional) to be the lead on that project, but this does not by itself move the actual work forward, he said. "For instance," he continued, "if I just put a project in Jira, it doesn't automatically make the project get done. I still have to go and make a case to [someone]. Well, that's the issue: where is the process there? Who do I make the case to?" He concluded that, given that some employees' work placed them in a position to start and complete many Jira tasks, whereas others' did not, "I would worry that it becomes a sort of a game at who's best at using Jira."

Still, by the end of August 2005 Rosedale had let everyone know that they must use either Jira or As & Os, but not both. The week before this announcement, forty-nine As & Os were sent (the company had about fifty-five employees at the time). The following week (the

Monday of which coincided with his announcement), twenty-four As & Os were sent, and the next week, thirteen. By January 2006 seven As & Os were being sent each week, on average. Employees had on the whole moved to incorporate the tool into their work practice whether they liked it or not. One who made the switch but then went back to writing As & Os after using Jira exclusively for about three months lamented how inconvenient it was to have to log into Jira to manage his list of tasks and his frustration at how Jira allowed only one level of subtasks (Jira tracked three things: "Bugs," "Tasks," and "Projects"; projects could have one level of subtasks). This employee cited the example of refitting the office to accommodate eighty-three people (the planned number of employees at the office in the near future). Because the task was both too large in scope over time and had too many layers of subtasks, it could not, in effect, exist in Jira.

Throughout 2005 Rosedale pushed ahead with efforts to use Jira to answer what I have noted was the central conundrum facing Linden Lab as a company: What to do next? Again, in the absence of legitimate and explicit vertical authority, the company had to find another means by which to generate politically legitimate (that is, plausibly horizontal) judgments for Linden Lab's priorities. For Rosedale, the first mechanism that occurred to him was *voting*. It was trivial to add a voting system to Jira, which allowed Lindens to vote on those projects they felt were most important, and this was done almost immediately. Variations on the system of voting (for a time, all employees were asked to vote for projects each week) continued throughout the year, with objections to the legitimacy of the results often grounded not only in the gap between what tasks Jira could see and the whole set of those done at the company but also on the system being "gameable"; that is, it invited vote-lobbying. Again, the possible incursion of connections (social capital), and perhaps credentials, was held to be a tainting influence on what would ideally be the act of an isolated individual: voting. One attempt to work around this problem was to draw on game design techniques to make a game out of picking "winners" in Jira. This effort is discussed in the next chapter.[4] Here, however, I would like to return to the issue of tools and governance by examining a set of Jira tasks surrounding a contentious issue: the implementation of point-to-point (P2P) teleportation in Second Life.

Getting the Point

I earlier mentioned two books that, in addition to Neal Stephenson's *Snow Crash*, circulated around Linden Lab and were often cited in conversations and the Friday lunches: Malone's *The Future of Work* (2004) and Surowiecki's *The Wisdom of Crowds* (2004). But it is interesting to consider another book that informed work practice there, from which people at Linden Lab took quite a different kind of lesson. That book was Jane Jacobs's landmark treatment of urban life and the failures of twentieth-century urban planning in the United States, *The Death and Life of Great American Cities* (1961).

Jane Jacobs upended conventional wisdom about city planning by arguing that the accidental, contingent, and emergent effects that cities could generate at the neighborhood level contributed the most to their security and vitality. As residents moved about, unavoidably somewhat inefficiently, from place to place, they were thrown into contact with things they would otherwise not find—the charming flower shop, the new dry cleaners, the newsstand. What is more, many of those involved in these encounters were in a position to monitor potential dangers (querying the loiterer, challenging the owner of the double-parked car). It was the accidental inefficiency of a city like New York, she argued, that made it the greatest city in the world. Urban planning that sought to eliminate this diversity created silent and insecure neighborhoods through its emphasis on single-use housing projects, large, car-dependent thoroughfares, and segregated commercial centers. This critical point of view is now the hallmark of today's New Urbanism, which sees Jacobs as something like a prophet. For Linden Lab, faced with the challenge of creating vibrant social life in Second Life, Jacobs' recommendations hit home. They also seemed at first glance utterly consistent with the points of view of Malone and Surowiecki (and, more broadly, we can recognize, the New Communalists): Jacobs emphasized the evolving processes that generated social goods in mixed-use neighborhoods.

But there was a problem. For how could Linden Lab achieve a similar situation in its own "urban planning" for Second Life, when there was no long history of local developments drawing on a mixed-use model in place in their world? The older neighborhoods of New York and other cities, after all, were built that way because their residents were in their cultural practice following models imported, for the most part, from Europe. For Linden Lab, the situation was different. Concerned about balkanization of the users within Second Life—just the kind of nonvital circumstance that Jacobs identified the failings of— they sought to *contrive* the contingent experience that Jacobs outlined. New Yorkers, she suggested, by needing to move about to reach their workplaces, encountered the efforts of others that they would not have otherwise sought out (often as pedestrians, even if briefly before and after riding the subway), and thereby came later to use and appreciate them. How could Linden Lab make use of the same mechanism to prompt a vital social life in Second Life? The answer, in part, was telehubs.

Second Life's grid is composed of hundreds (then thousands) of squares, or sims, each housed on a server (some dual core servers housed two sims). To move locally in Second Life, avatars can walk about; or ride in vehicles such as motorcycles, cars, and planes (and stranger creations); or fly. These means of locomotion are relatively slow, however, if one wants to move across many sims. Originally (that is, for a short time after Second Life launched in June 2003), users could teleport from any point on the grid to any other point, a capability referred to as point-to-point, or P2P.[5] Linden Lab installed telehubs several months after launch in an effort to promote the kind of community life that Jacobs lauded. Users could still teleport *from* any point in the grid, and they could indicate any point as their destination, but they would arrive at the nearest telehub to their destination.[6] Each telehub served as a common arrival point for several sims, and its structure was created by the content team. The user would arrive and, by looking around, see a "beacon" (a vertical beam of red extending into the sky) indicating their desired destination. The idea was that users would, in the course of moving (typically, flying) to their destination, encounter in a contingent fashion other content in Second Life—shops, performance spaces, entertainment venues, beautiful "builds," and the like.

Telehubs succeeded in a sense, because land values around them rose to reflect their desirability as a place to connect with users. Some telehubs became recognizable destinations in their own right. It seemed that Linden Lab had succeeded in accomplishing a contradiction: contriving a healthy civil society that was supposed to emerge without contrivance (at least in Jacobs's example of New York City). But there were problems. The primary of these was that users *knew* that P2P teleportation was possible (even trivial) to provide. After all, it was common knowledge that it had existed originally, and Lindens working in world, who had exclusive access to "god tools," had P2P as well. For many users, their individual interest in arriving directly at their destination overran a civic interest which seemed, at best, vague. Moreover, a technical problem plagued many telehubs. The large amount of development around them (including not only buildings but "scripted" objects, such as rotating signs and the like) took a fair amount of time to appear on the teleporter's computer—arriving at a telehub often meant arriving at an almost empty space, with the destination beacon in clear view. Only on beginning to fly toward the destination might one bump into invisible barriers—the walls of buildings next to the telehub that were only beginning to "rez in." This was a source of great annoyance to many users. In addition, some users had created scripted devices (such as one called ROAM) which would fly users (usually, their own customers for specific shops and other destinations) at a very rapid pace, and without the danger of collisions, from telehubs to destinations.

Over the course of 2005 Rosedale, as the public voice of Linden Lab, spent a fair amount of time defending the telehubs. I was able to witness firsthand a face-to-face discussion with about a dozen users who had made a "pilgrimage" to Linden Lab (though they had not come to pursue this issue specifically). In it, Rosedale relied heavily on the approach from Jacobs to make the case for the continued importance of the telehubs, but eventually the technical problems and user pressure led Linden Lab in August 2005 to begin considering whether to implement P2P for some or all users. Much of this discussion took place through Jira, and while I did not obtain permission to quote from the comments accompanying Jira tasks, I can summarize the sequence of proposals and subsequent debate.

The first Jira-initiated discussion (there is a comment area below every Jira task) was by Rosedale, who provides a lengthy description (more than sixteen hundred words) of his reasoning on why the telehubs must be abandoned. After citing Jacobs' ideas as the impetus for their implementation, he lists the above shortcomings and then adds a few more observations, such as the fact that telehubs, chosen a priori by Linden Lab, do not move dynamically to nearby, higher-density locations. Another issue for him was the desirability of letting landowners set a specific spot as the local arrival point—users arriving from a telehub often would have trouble finding the "entrance" to their destination, as the red beacon was often centered on the building or other structure. He goes on to suggest that simply standing in Second Life, with a 128 meter viewing distance available in every direction, should be enough to satisfy Jacobs's ideal of bringing people into contact with possibly unexpected diversions.

Further discussions about the issue in Jira (and in e-mail and other media) focused on some of the technical challenges in providing P2P (all the "stuff"—scripted objects—that some users might have with them might strain server resources or cause other bugs or slowdowns), as well as the question of whether this should be a "premium" feature, available only to those who continued to pay a monthly subscription fee (which gave them the right to own land). A vote was held through the vote system that had been coded into Jira, and P2P for all was approved, with its implementation achieved at the end of 2005. There were vocal negative reactions from users, the most eloquent of which came from Gwyneth Llewelyn (2005; Llewelyn is a Second Life name), who posted an essay on her blog in late November 2005 in response to the imminent P2P. There Llewelyn noted how one of the primary effects of the introduction of P2P was economic—many of the most wealthy Second Life users were "land barons," a large proportion of whom relied on rental income from businesses on their land next to telehubs. She also raised the possibility that a small but vocal minority had called for P2P and lamented the inability of individuals to maintain a self-interest sufficiently enlightened to see the telehubs' value despite their inconvenience. Hard feelings about the issue persisted for some time.

In the end, P2P is a lesson in the extent and limits of Linden Lab's control over Second Life and the constant challenge of providing affordances that would support the growth of the community, just as the staff similarly sought to support their growth as a company. The transition to Jira from As & Os never sat well with some employees at Linden Lab, who felt the new technological conditions of their work ran counter to an established and flexible practice already in place. In telehubs, we can see a similar imposition of a technological change, with consequences that upended the existing social arrangements of power. Rosedale commented on this predicament in an interview with me, immediately following the announcement of P2P. In it, as Brand did in his *Catalog*, he felt drawn to the analogy of the divine:

> We can't use global contrivances . . . to motivate social behavior. I mean, I increasingly believe that that is *not* a position that we can take. . . . I think one of the most powerful statements that can be made about this stuff is the repurposing of the Lawrence Lessig statement, you know, code is law. And I think that code is *physical* law, or code is god, is also the right thing to say about something like Second Life.
>
> . . .
>
> The way that we will reach into the world and effect change is by altering [code] . . . and in the light of, say, imagining more of an open source environment in the future, that means we'll ultimately have to convince other people to actually accept our changes, but— only by changing the code. We only speak to the world through the code.

Jira and the multiple other tools that Lindens used were seen around Linden Lab as tools in the sense given above: they were useful and value-neutral means of tapping into individual judgment and aggregating it to arrive at legitimate decisions. Fond of saying that under an ideal company structure he would cease to exist, Rosedale in discourse represented the aspiration that practically underwrote the dual projects of Second Life *and* Linden Lab as sites for individual, autonomous creativity for whom technology was a handmaiden. Missing from this representation is the degree to which it depended on a particular and political point of view, but for the purposes of this chapter what is just as significant is the way this representation ignored two further alignments: first, how governing Linden Lab paralleled the struggles (in legitimacy, in scale) of governing Second Life; and second, how faith in the tool-making tool of computer programming practice served as the go-to practical means by which a public policy problem could be answered.

3_KNOWING THE GAMER
FROM THE GAME

The day wears on at Linden Lab's Second Street office in March 2005. As five o'clock approaches, I see a developer here, a marketing person there, start to gather personal possessions and head home for the day. But the room is still mostly full as the first shout rings through the air: "Yes!" Some scattered laughter follows, and a quick look around the room shows about six Lindens, their faces illuminated by the swiftly moving and colorful graphics on their monitors, sitting in the classic PC gamer pose: one hand on mouse, another with fingers poised over the w, a, s, and d keys of the keyboard. I glance at the nearby screen of a member of the QA team, and catch a brief glimpse of futuristic guns firing and armored avatars running around a hilly landscape, with many objects and buildings around as available cover. This is not the comparatively placid Second Life landscape—it is a game of Tribes: Vengeance, a multiplayer online game that allows two teams (of up to sixteen players) to play Capture the Flag and other contests while equipped with powerful weapons, armor, and jetpacks (these allow players to fly for a short distance). The generally dark environment of Linden Lab adds to the atmosphere; as one Linden put it, "It [makes] the Tribes games kind of eerie. . . . Shouting, you know, and . . . all these screens with action on them."

I later learn that there have been a number of games that have occupied the role of end-of-the-day diversion, and in interviews with Linden employees it was clear that many of them considered themselves committed gamers. Those who did not, correspondingly, often went out of their way to mention it to me and how it related to hearing about Linden Lab ("I'm not a gamer, so I just got a forward with about twelve [job] postings"), being interested in Second Life ("I thought it was gaming . . . that just sound[ed] too game geeky"), and using Second Life ("I kept bumping against the wall and I couldn't figure out the spatial things—I wasn't game-savvy enough,"). These comments were, by and large, the exception—gaming was part of Linden Lab practice. The category of the "office game" existed as a social fact around Linden Lab. As Cory Ondrejka put it in a comment he contributed to a Web log discussion (Combs 2006):

> [Members of] the core development team [the earliest members of the company] . . . were fairly serious FPS [first-person shooter], console, and other game players. Counter-Strike was the office game for nearly three years. My background was arcade, combat/race, and race games, all about as far removed from MMOs as you could get.

The online office game was supplemented by offline games, the most popular of which was the Nerf battle—many Lindens kept loaded Nerf brand guns (which shoot small, polyurethane foam rockets) close at hand. At any moment (though more likely toward the end of the day or just before lunch) a Nerf battle could break out. There were also a number of games available to play in the gaming room, including a number of gaming consoles (PlayStation2, Xbox), "stand up" arcade games (Street Fighter II, Galaga), and a pool table (after moving to the larger, Sansome Street location). What is more, a good number of Lindens came to the company, like Ondrejka, from game development backgrounds. Of the approximately fifty regular employees (that is, not counting contractors) in early May 2005, about twenty had some professional background in games, whether computer games or others, and this number was disproportionately high among developers (a group of about fifteen at the time).

Of course, Tribes was quite different from Second Life in some ways. Its environment was not a persistent world (its games began and ended), it could not accommodate more than thirty-two users, and there was a narrower scope for user creation. But the two pieces of software shared a number of important characteristics, and these are most obviously seen in the interface itself. In both of them one controls an avatar via the combined use of the mouse and the keyboard. The mouse selects/targets/interacts with objects in the environment as well as on-screen buttons and menus and controls the view (the "camera"). The keyboard is used for movement ("w" for forward, "a" for left turn or to slide-step or "strafe" left, "d" for right turn or to strafe right, "s" to move backwards, and the space bar to jump) and for "hot keys"— other keys on the keyboard that instantly activate certain abilities or use certain items. This interface was pioneered in a specific genre of computer games called "first-person shooter," and it emphasizes rapid movement of the avatar (to evade others' attacks as much as to get the player from place to place) in combination with the ability to target things in the environment. These games can be multiplayer, in which case at least part of the game involves targeting and/or collaborating with other players, but they can also be single player games, in which the player targets enemies controlled by the software ("nonplayer characters," or NPCs).

Additionally, Tribes, like Second Life, has a "physics"; that is, it has what is called in the gaming industry a "physics engine." This is the part of the game's software that applies a set of behaviors to objects (including avatars) in the environment about how they move as a result of "impact" or "gravity" or the like. In Second Life, as in Tribes, if you bump against an object, your avatar "bounces" back in a way analogous to offline experience. Similarly, if you throw an object down a hill, it bounces and rolls until it comes to a stop.

Already we can notice that Second Life users with experience in PC games of this type come to Second Life with some cultural capital— they are competent, to some degree, in moving about the space and in interacting with its objects according to the local physics (in a sense). For users unfamiliar with this interface, failures of social performance exhibit themselves in stop-and-start moving, walking into walls, and the like and are easily recognizable to other users. For users that come from other games it is the subtle differences that prompt failures, at least for a time. Second Life has no dedicated "strafe" keys (often, in other virtual worlds, "q" and "e"), so when I enter Second Life after having spent time in another virtual world, such as World of Warcraft, I do not move elegantly. The primary point, however, is that Second Life owes a great deal to games in just this distinctive interface. But the relationships between Second Life, Linden Lab, and games go much deeper, and to sort them out we must first begin by seeing games in a different way from that to which we are accustomed.

When I earlier discussed how things came to be at stake in Second Life and other virtual worlds, I pointed out that the possibility of failure as much as the persistence of the environment made this possible. But to speak about what people do in places like Second Life, and the consequences of that, in terms of success and failure is actually too narrow. It is too narrow because it makes everything seem to depend on users' or players' agency, and specifically their performance in relation to their intentions. But what we need to be able to do is to talk about the effects of user's actions in these spaces in a way that encompasses even the *unintended consequences* of what they do—results that may not be success *or* failures but may be consequential nonetheless (Giddens 1984). At times, after all, these new outcomes are innovations that have a lasting impact on practice (although I have no idea whether my accidental discovery of how to make a dome appear to be covered in hammered copper has lived on anywhere but in my own mind).

In addition, we need to be able to accommodate the fact that outcomes are shaped not just by what people do, accidentally or intentionally, but by other processes in play, as in the way that, for example, the weather shapes outcomes in everyday life. We need to be able to talk about the reasons why, in the course of events, things can simply go another way. What are the sources of this indeterminacy of social process, and how are they present in virtual worlds as the result of design or accident? The emergent effects that complex spaces like virtual worlds generate depend on this open-endedness, the lack of determinacy in the environment and participants' actions in it, and this open-endedness is to a certain extent contrived.

In a sense, this is similar to what the New Communalists recognized about the collective effects of human action over time amid an array of material affordances—the way that system-level effects grow out of a complex array of microactivities. But after recognizing the existence of unpredictable effects, they took a further, normative step that portrayed emergent effects as *legitimate* by virtue of being emergent. But we need not take that step—in fact, I am striving here to distinguish my take on emergence from theirs on that point—to appreciate that the open-endedness of Second Life and places like it—the way they are complex enough to generate contingent outcomes—bears closer inspection. Once we do that, we start to recognize that the roots of *architecting* that open-endedness lie in games and in the techniques of game design that some Lindens brought to bear on both Second Life and Linden Lab itself. What we see is the appearance of a perhaps unexpected distinction between two types of makers—the makers of the game and the makers of the environment for the game.

The Elements of Gameness

There is a standard account of what games are that saturates both popular and academic accounts of games. This is the idea that games are a subset of "play," where play is understood to be something fundamentally opposed to "work." The primary shortcoming of seeing games as play, and play as opposed to work, is that games become domains intrinsically set apart from everyday experience.[1] As separate, safe (consequence-free), and pleasurable (or, conversely, dangerously seductive), games in this view stand as something very different from people's day-to-day life (with its "real" stakes, a distressing unwillingness to stay compartmentalized, and ample supply of both pain and pleasure). But to look at games differently is to see how their ability to command human attention may be the result of quite the opposite—it is what games *share* with everyday experience that accounts for how they engage us.

What do they share? At root, games share the mixture of pattern and indeterminacy that also characterizes human experience, no matter how routinized or chaotic that experience can at times be. It is this that makes games seem to occupy an almost oppositional position with respect to bureaucracy, as I suggested in the introduction. Here is a definition to work from:

> *A game is a semibounded and socially legitimate domain of contrived contingency that generates interpretable outcomes.*

By "contrived contingency" I mean the mixture of constraint and open-endedness that all games have. All games are relatively separate (the degree of separation is highly context-dependent—it is a cultural accomplishment) and socially condoned arenas. In them, one or more sources of indeterminacy (or the proper philosophical term, contingency) are present along with certain constraints; together and over time these generate contingent or indeterminate outcomes. These outcomes are subject to interpretation—in this way games can generate meaning.

When we consider the matter for a moment, we can see that games are distinguished by their *legitimate* indeterminacy: at their start participants (and, possibly, spectators) accept the fact (in fact, they expect) that they do not know what the outcomes will be. Many games have a series of outcomes all along their playing out (the missed basketball shot, the dice roll in craps, the initial deal in bridge), and some games have no "end conditions" at all—they never end, such as role-playing games like Dungeons and Dragons. This is again not to say that games are unconstrained—they achieve a mixture of constraint and unpredictability, and this mixture generates outcomes that are then interpreted (winners and losers, yes, but also less dichotomous conclusions, such as whether a player has footfaulted in tennis).

But it is not enough that games through their playing out generate indeterminate outcomes that can be interpreted; after all, that would also be a fair characterization of much of our human experience. Games occupy *contrived* and *legitimate* spaces, and this legitimacy is generated socially, by participants and spectators (if there are any), as well as at times by institutions (such as the International Olympic Committee). This point bears repeating. Games are socially constructed by a shared commitment to their legitimacy as contrived spaces where indeterminate outcomes can unfold. Their contrivance furthermore makes games semibounded; that is, held to be in some *relative* sense separable from other domains of our experience, in a manner analogous to how, for example, courtrooms can be seen as imperfectly separate spaces.

One vital implication of this account of games, and it accords with what we see in games empirically, is that games are open-ended even with respect to their form. Games can change, and this can alter the conditions for further participation in them. In a word, games are in this respect characterized by *process* (they are *processual*)—they demonstrate the constant potential for change and reconfiguration.[2] The taking of professional American basketball "above the rim" by Oscar Robertson and Julius Irving is one example of how games can change as they are played, and the ability to "dribble out" time at the end of a game by Bob Cousy years earlier is another. These changes in practice can further lead to adjustments of constraints or possibilities (basketball's twenty-four second clock). Complicated questions of legitimacy arise as a result of this dynamic quality—when is a change legitimate and when does it turn a fair competition into something more like a confirmatory rite? I return to the question of legitimacy further on, but first we can pause for a moment and consider in a more fine-grained fashion just what kinds of constraints and indeterminacies constitute games.

As may be obvious already, the rules are only one part of the picture— games cannot be reduced to their rules. This is because the "rules" of a game are not like the rules of a bureaucracy, which are intended to reduce unpredictability across cases. Even if bureaucracies are unpredictable and inefficient in practice, their rules are of a different order from those of games because they are rationalized in the Weberian sense: they are supposed to produce regular, consistent outcomes (even if they fail in practice). The same might be said of most computer software code, such as that found in an income tax program. Dibbell (2006: 109) draws an interesting parallel between online games and such programs. While both make use of code and Internet connectivity, the income tax program is not designed to generate unpredictable outcomes. On the contrary, variations in its estimates of owed tax from one try to the next are an indication that something has gone quite wrong. Games, however, are about the opposite: they are about contriving and calibrating multiple contingencies and constraints to produce indeterminate (though perhaps patterned or expected) outcomes, which are then interpreted (made meaningful).[3]

The contrivance of these sources of unpredictability is achieved in part through the presence of various kinds of constraints, including but not only the rules. These constraints additionally include the architectural (encompassing the gamut of relatively non-negotiable and concrete constraints, from physical layout and landscape to the implicit code of online games); the cultural, such as social conventions (the set of practices and expectations that are often implicit and taken for granted); and the economic (the familiar constraints of the market in all its forms).[4] In this I follow Lessig (1999), among others, in seeing these four modes of control as the primary means by which we are constrained throughout our experience. Any game may contain one or more of these types of control, but unlike bureaucracies games evince a balance between these modes of control and various sources of contingency. Games are distinctive in their achievement of such a generative balance between the open-endedness of contingencies and the reproducibility of their conditions, and this is what makes the practice of game design useful to those who, like many at Linden Lab, want to find a way to govern via a means that rejects purely top-down control.[5]

Contingency is also a fruitful path to follow if we are interested in what makes games compelling. According to Heidegger and the phenomenologists, our existence in an uncertain world not of our own making is a fundamental aspect of human experience. For the pragmatists, this uncertainty extended to pure contingency, the assertion that the universe did not simply *seem* unpredictable because of our own imperfect ability (now or perhaps ever) to grasp its nevertheless determinate processes but *was* indeterminate (see Menand 2001). In this respect the wide-ranging indeterminacy of our everyday experience and the contrived indeterminacy of games point toward a bridge, rather than a gap, between games and other aspects of our lives.

By *contingency* (or indeterminacy—I use them interchangeably here) I mean *that which could have been otherwise*; that is, that which was *not necessary* (or determined) in a philosophical sense. The potential sources of contingency that are found in games are the same sources we encounter throughout our lives. They are just relatively (though not perfectly) bounded in a game. That games have this fundamental quality of multilayered indeterminacy allows them both to mimic and constitute everyday experience, and this is what makes well-designed games compelling. The unfolding of contingent outcomes in games commands our attention because it presents just the right mix of the expected and the unexpected (provided the game is well-designed, whether by a game designer or by historical practice). A game that is too predictable becomes routine and uninteresting. A game that is too unpredictable becomes frustrating and uninteresting. Game designers are notable for their ability to calibrate these unpredictabilities to engage the participant and make the experience compelling (I am avoiding more explicitly or obviously valenced normative terms such as "enjoyable"). Making a "balanced" game (as it is termed in game design) is about creating the complex, implicit, contingent conditions wherein the texture of engaged human experience can happen.

If the contrivance of contingency is a defining feature of games, what kinds of indeterminacy are involved? Or, rather, from where does the indeterminacy come? The most familiar source of contingency in games is *stochastic contingency* (what the philosopher Alasdair MacIntyre called "pure contingency"; 1984: 99–100). This is the randomness produced by, for example, a well-shuffled deck of cards or a tossed die. Here, unpredictable outcomes spring forth as the result of a process sufficiently complex as to produce chaotic results. Some of the oldest archaeological finds are objects of this kind: bones, dice, or lots. Other less obvious (more implicit) examples of sources of stochastic contingency in games include the weather at a baseball game or other sporting event, participants' illness or injury, and "lag" in an online game as a result of high Internet traffic. It becomes easy (and important) to recognize that stochastic unpredictability can be generated by explicit, contrived means (dice, wheels of fortune) but also generated by means beyond the control of the game's participants. This is further confirmation of how the separability of games is not absolute; games, by their design, can achieve at best only a relative separation from other parts of experience. More recently, this form of contingency in games, specifically computer games, has been steadily transformed away from previously predominant explicit mechanisms, such as dice, and toward implicit stochastic generation.[6]

Another source of contingency is *social contingency* (MacIntyre calls this "game-theoretic" contingency; 1984: 97–99). This is the indeterminacy of never being certain about another's point of view (and often, resources), a key component of chess, poker, and countless other games. The extent to which (economic) game theory has focused on differences in information is a reflection of the correct recognition of social contingency as a factor in games, but it is never the only source of contingency. The challenge involves not simply making accurate guesses about others' points of view but acting on those guesses, and that leads to a third source of contingency, *performative contingency*. Here the issue is the execution of an action by a participant, an action that may succeed or fail. This kind of indeterminacy plays a most obvious role in athletic contests and is the core of many action-oriented computer games, but it is present in all games. It is the avenue by which a player's actions influence the outcomes (if sometimes in unexpected ways). At times this performance is embodied and rapid, such as in FPS games; at other times, it is simply about not making errors in following game procedures, such as in counting the proper spaces in a game of Monopoly. In a way, all our actions in games, as in life, are performative in this sense; they run the risk of success, failure, or some new result that demands an accounting (an innovation or exploit? See Consalvo 2007). Games call on you to perform, to accomplish the actions that give you the best opportunity to succeed in the game, even if the definition of success is itself a moving target.

This moving target signals a different source of contingency in games, and that is their *semiotic contingency*, the indeterminacy of meaning in them. Outcomes may always challenge existing schemes of interpretation and lead to new meanings. In addition to the changing game of basketball noted above (which prompted never-before confronted questions about whether dribbling out "should" be legal, for example), Bobby Fischer's match against Boris Spassky was another case where the meaning of the game was transformed by its context. Jesse Owens at the 1936 Olympics is another—the meaning of any given gaming outcome is not set in stone.[7] The complex contingency of today's large-scale online games has powerful effects on meaning, conceived here as always arising from the meeting point of existing, shared interpretive frameworks and unique, contingent circumstances. Additionally, as games themselves show most powerfully, the shared engagement of contingency is a powerful means for the development of trust and belonging. Together these implications suggest that, if a domain is rich enough in possibilities, it can generate for its users a distinctive disposition (Mauss and Bourdieu's *habitus*) about how to act within it.

Defining games as, first and foremost, contrived forums for the generation of indeterminacy avoids the normative judgments contained in the modernist (i.e., work vs. play) account of games. Instead, and crucially, *it places game contexts and other arenas of human experience ontologically on a par with each other.* Everyday experience and game arenas, each filled with uncertainties, can inform each other through metaphor, but they can also both be the site for real stakes and real consequences. Gaming becomes sensible not as an escape from everyday life but as just one of its multiform domains, an activity that is compelling precisely because, like life, it presents ongoing, unpredictable outcomes to its players that challenge them to perform. The only difference is that the game presents multiple contingencies in a relatively bounded, explicit, legitimate, and perhaps more readily graspable form, one that is the product of design.

It bears restating, however, that I am not, by this emphasis on games as sites for the generation of contingent outcomes, proposing that games (or life!) are not largely marked by regularities, patterns, recurrences, and reproductions, whether of institutions, practices, or meanings. It is only that any view of games that makes the crucial mistake of forgetting that their contingency, however minimal, is always present, takes an inevitable step toward a mistaken conclusion. It separates them from the rest of our experience and undercuts what makes them compelling, powerful, and consequential, just as any deterministic account of social change founders on the accidents and contingencies that undoubtedly play a role in history.

Task Masters

This approach to games makes it easier for us to recognize the place that games occupied for Turner's New Communalists. It is an issue about which he provides some tantalizing details, and we can use them to expand our understanding of how games relate to the problem of authority for Linden Lab and more generally for the emerging institutions of the digital age. "[Ken] Kesey and the Pranksters turned to various devices to distribute and, ostensibly, level . . . power. One of the devices was a simple spinner. The Pranksters regularly played a game in which a number of them would sit in a circle. Someone would spin the spinner, and whoever it pointed to would then have full power over the group for the next thirty minutes" (Turner 2006: 65). Ken Kesey and the Merry Pranksters were close to Stewart Brand and strongly associated with the New Communalist counterculture of the 1960s. When they turned to stochastic contingency for their game of authority, they were incorporating both a source of indeterminacy—the spinner—and a constraining rule that interpreted the spinner's outcome and dictated an arrangement of power. Another example is a game they played with the *I Ching*; a person would toss a set of coins and then consult the book for a correlating bit of text, which would then be taken as guiding action.[8] Turner is right to zero in on the denial of authority these games necessarily involve (Turner 2006: 65):

The spinner and the *I Ching* did serve to take power out of the hands of designated leaders. If the former turned group members into followers, it did so only temporarily, and only with the members' consent. If the latter threw up an obscure ancient fortune, it also demanded that one work out its meaning on one's own. In both cases, the individual remained empowered. But within the context of the Pranksters, these devices also served an ideological function. That is, they not only distributed some power among group members and decision-making devices, but they also diverted attention from the very real and centralized leadership Kesey was exerting. . . . Kesey and the Pranksters did everything they could to deny the fact of concentrated power in their midst. In a pattern that would become familiar around the digital technologies of the 1990s, they reassigned it . . . to devices.

I would make a friendly amendment to this conclusion, however. It was not in devices—in technology alone—that the Pranksters sought to invest authority. The account of games I have given above allows us to recognize that they sought to invest power in gamelike *processes*, aided by technology. It was *game design* that they engaged in—the combining of constraining rules and sources of indeterminacy (the coins, the spinner)—and this was a harbinger of what was to come.[9] Kesey and Pranksters had only familiar, "analog" sources of stochastic contingency ready to hand, the accessible computers that followed soon after allowed for a vast multiplication of both controls and contingencies.

Thus, what the example of Kesey and the Pranksters should lead us to consider is the nature of individual agency *in* a game as it relates the authority to *make* a game. Allow me to explain. A core idea exemplified in the *Whole Earth Catalog* was of an individual, amid a complex system of affordances, pursuing enlightened self-interest and contributing to collective and emergent effects that were thereby legitimate. In this view, authority is collectively generated out of many individuated acts of agency within a system. With the spinner and *I Ching* games the Pranksters sought to contrive that circumstance. That is, they sought not only to provide "tools" to people in the unbounded world of the everyday but to set up a circumstance of constraints and possibilities *within which* that individual pursuit of enlightened self-interest would take place. But something very important changes when the aim is no longer simply the provision of tools but rather the broader project of contriving (and providing) the conditions—the system, in a sense—in which those affordances are encountered and used. We might say that in this the Pranksters, like current virtual world makers, sought to have their authority and eat it, too.

For Linden Lab, this was not simply an opposition between themselves as game makers and their users as game players, however. Like the Pranksters, this gaming of authority characterized their relationships within the company. Given the way in which the same ideals informed their attempts to govern themselves, we can begin to explore how games came to be used around Linden Lab, and what this had to do with the employees' puzzle of authority over themselves. The way in which Jira offered a wide scope for customization meant that it was an avenue through which the application of game design technique could find a footing. In mid-2005 there was one particularly revealing effort, through a turn to both computer programming and techniques from games, that constituted a practical answer to Linden Lab's political dilemma: how to make legitimate collective decisions that accorded with a disposition both highly individualized and characterized by a high degree of faith in technology. This was the implementation of a chess ranking system to generate out of Jira a list of the most important tasks for the company.

Chess ranking systems are one application of "Elo rating systems," a group of algorithmic methods for calculating the relative skill levels of large numbers of players for two-player games. Based on a system developed originally by Arpad Elo (1978) for generating a ranking of chess players, they have since been both modified and improved within chess and adapted for other two-player games. The challenge that generates the need for this system for chess is twofold. On one hand, there is an interest in measuring and ranking players relative to one another. On the other, the game itself involves only two players, and these players are dispersed in space (and in time), so there is no perfect opportunity for all possible players to compete and determine who is the best.

What is more, absolute skill cannot be observed; it can only be inferred from wins, losses, and draws. A ranking system generates a rating for each player and is seen as legitimate in the degree to which these ratings seem to accord with the matches that do get played. Thus a key aim of these systems is also to predict the outcomes of matches between rated players, and its accuracy is thereby judged (and thereby the system may also be modified). In this way, Elo rating systems generate an *emergent* ordered ranking, and this emergent quality made this technique an attractive solution for the challenge that faced Linden Lab: if the right game could be designed, the Elo system could be used to generate a ranked order of prioritization from a heterogenous collection of company tasks. It would also have the important effect of encouraging voting by being "fun"—despite Friday presentations and other encouragement by Rosedale to vote on Jira tasks, the voting system was "underused" (as a Linden in marketing put it to me).[10]

In June 2005 one developer at Linden Lab, quite familiar with chess ranking systems, set about to code onto Jira such a game. Pitting two (and only two) tasks against each other for Lindens to choose, the results of these "matches" would automatically be plugged into a version of the Elo ranking system and over time generate a list of highest-ranked to lowest-ranked Jira tasks. Rosedale enthusiastically supported this effort, and in two days the programmer had created the system and sent an e-mail over the company e-mail list containing a link to a Web site where employees could participate. Upon arriving at the site, one saw a simple presentation of two Jira tasks, including each one's title, unique Jira number, and a brief description. Employees were simply to pick one (the "more important") of the two (or pick a "draw"—they could also push a "don't understand" button for either task), and the system would record that match result and immediately refresh the page with another match of two more tasks.

Many Lindens tried out the system with some enthusiasm, as it seemed relatively resistant to vote lobbying (seen as a problem for their first attempts to incorporate voting into Jira). Hundreds of matches were "played" in a short span of time (a matter of days), and a ranked list was generated. For Rosedale, this was a step on the road toward realizing an ideal of company decision making from the ground up. For others, the system was suspect at the point of participation; presented with two entirely heterogenous tasks (add a urinal to the men's bathroom versus add a Web browser to the Second Life client), they felt that picking between them was nonsensical. Whereas more direct systems of voting foundered on problems of exploitation (vote lobbying), this one foundered on heterogeneity. It is also important to mention that the developer himself was skeptical of whether this system would generate legitimately ranked company priorities. For him, this was something that was worth trying and interesting as an exercise. It was eventually abandoned in practice, and other initiatives to tap into the wisdom of Linden Lab's crowd were tried.

The turn to a game system in concert with programming technique reveals a great deal about how Linden Lab's paradox of political control and political aspirations was confronted in practice (Kelty 2005, Coleman 2004). As an anti-institutional space, Second Life was designed to be open-ended for its users to allow for creativity but not so wide open as to leave them with an overwhelming (perhaps even paralyzing) sense of possibility. Game mechanics were an attractive solution for Linden Lab because games generate outcomes not through vertical directives, nor through individual cheating (provided controls against "gaming the system" are in place), but as the result of a complex and open-ended set of processes resting at least in part on individual performance. It is but a small step to see these outcomes as inherently legitimate and consonant with the political attitudes that Turner and others have outlined.

But Linden Lab did not thereby achieve escape velocity from the puzzle of authority. Just like the case of the Pranksters, we can recognize how this turn to games ultimately generates a distinction between the agency provided the game's players and the standing authority of the game makers, who set the conditions under which the game takes place. This has important implications for how Second Life users (and, indeed, the human in general) were imagined around Linden Lab. But the approach to what games are that I have laid out only gets us so far in attempting to pursue these implications. This is because we must also delve into how game players themselves were imagined around Linden Lab. It turns out that Lindens imagined themselves and their users as a particular kind of gamer, and therefore favored a particular kind of game, one that accorded with the technoliberal ideology that reigned around Linden Lab. We can begin to understand this picture of the gamer by looking more closely at what ideas underwrite the "gamer" in the Western cultural imagination.

Homo Lindens

Most engineers ... consider themselves to be professionals ... and ... engineers do have a professional code. Among its tenets is the general idea that the engineer's right environment is a highly structured one, in which only right and wrong answers exist. It's a binary world; the computer might be its paradigm. And many engineers seem to aspire to be binary people within it. No wonder. The prospect is alluring. (Kidder 1981: 146–147)

While the picture that Kidder provides of man the engineer rang true to a certain extent for me around Linden Lab, what is missing from it in thinking about how the human was imagined around Linden Lab, even given the prevailing influence of its computer engineers, is games. Linden Lab's engineers were gamers and saw games, in all their indeterminacy, as not incompatible with the notion of a godlike figure designing an entire world. What happens when *homo ludens* meets *homo creans*?

Johan Huizinga set the tone for much of the inquiry into games and society in the latter half of the twentieth century with his book *Homo Ludens* (1955). In it he did much to contribute to the unfortunate view of games as separate and consequence-free (see 1955: 10–12; developed more rigidly still by Caillois [1961]), but as with many such mid-century works of cultural history, illuminating contradictions abound. As Huizinga's argument develops and he reaches the end of his text, he seems to focus on something quite different: "Civilization is, in its earliest phases, played. It does not come *from* play . . . it arises *in* and *as* play, and never leaves it" (1955: 173). Huizinga is much more enlightening when he speaks of the "play-element" (a type of experience or disposition), rather than of "play" as a (separable, safe) activity. The play-element for Huizinga is marked by an interest in uncertainty and the challenge to perform that arises in competition, and he opposed it above all to utilitarianism and the drive for efficiency. This play-element is marked by the legitimacy of improvisation and innovation that it allows. Caillois, despite his misleading claim that games are occasions of "pure waste," similarly recognized the centrality of contingency in games (see his discussion of *alea*; 1961). The fact that games legitimize failure (as often cited in discussions of their advantages for learning; see Gee 2003) is a consequence of this legitimate indeterminacy. Huizinga felt that the play element was on the wane in western civilization since the eighteenth century (see also Dibbell 2006: 59–60), threatened by the drive for efficiency (and in this way he in part foreshadows my own contrast between bureaucracy and games).

Play as a mode of experience was productively explored further by Csikszentmihalyi (1990), who found that this disposition could be found wherever people faced an ongoing mixture of pattern and unpredictability that demanded a practiced mastery of performance (what he calls "flow), such as a factory worker who happens to confront the properly engaging mixture of constraint and (perhaps dangerous) possibility in manipulating multiple machines and objects. Practiced makers of cedar shingles, for example, deftly handle the slight variations in every piece of wood that comes their way as they coordinate their bodily movements in extremely close proximity to two open and spinning saws. The focus on a state of mastery that one finds in Csikszentmihalyi leaves us in a less than an ideal position from which to recognize much play experience, because so much of human experience in games takes place before such mastery is achieved (if it ever is).

On the way to mastery, the experience of playing a game is perhaps best characterized as *learning*, in the broad sense (see Gee 2003). It is a situation where each new moment may bring new circumstances, new information, and that novelty needs to be incorporated (often in the literal sense) into the player's practice and understanding. It is, in short, a readiness to improvise, and it therefore demands an attitude perhaps best described as pragmatic.[11] Louis Menand notes how Oliver Wendell Holmes characterized the pragmatic approach to knowledge as making a "bet" on the behavior of the universe (2001: 217), a universe that was in Menand's words "charged with indeterminacy" and therefore never perfectly knowable (195). More recently, a number of social theorists have also felt drawn to the metaphor of games, bets, and risk taking to describe how human beings experience an always-changing world.[12] This approach to social life is quite consistent with pragmatic thought, in that it seeks to capture the ongoing and open-ended nature of human experience while recognizing the ongoing influence of rulelike constraints on our actions. These kinds of connections suggest that games, properly understood, have a great deal to teach us about the history of social thought, but I leave further (and incomplete) wrangling of this weighty subject to its own venue.

To a certain extent, then, when many Lindens imagined their users, they imagined game players in this sense. But, and this is vital to note, these were gamers in a highly individualistic sense. For many Lindens a game constituted, at root, a challenge to an *individual* to act within an open-ended system, whether that game involved other players or not, and this logic applied to themselves as well. In this way, their idea of games effectively emphasized their performative contingencies at the expense of their social and semiotic dimensions. Consider how vote lobbying constituted a problem for their initial efforts to generate ranked lists out of Jira through a straight voting system. Vote lobbying contradicted their aims because it introduced "social" elements (social capital, and cultural capital in the form of credentials) that, in their view, corrupted the process. The irony is that such promotion and persuasion was undoubtedly a part of how work was moved forward under the previous As & Os system. This is, on pause, quite remarkable, because it even suggests an almost complete rejection of open debate or discussion in the Habermasian sense (Habermas 1987; this is again consistent with what Kelty has argued about the nondiscursive politics of computer programming [2005]). Instead, the ideal was a game in which players each performed within a contrived system, and did so individually. Even randomness (stochastic indeterminacy) was included only insofar as it provided a bulwark against outwitting the game system's attempt to provide a properly limited situation in which to perform (as in the apparently random selection of Jira tasks). Humans performing in this way in such contrived systems epitomized "gamers" around Linden Lab. Only the effects of their aggregate efforts could be trusted.

There is another important issue here. To self-identify as a gamer around Linden Lab (and, I would suggest, more broadly in the current moment) is not only to claim an affinity for games and to think primarily in terms of individual challenge. It is typically to identify oneself as someone with a preference for *these kinds* of games, and not others. As scholars of so-called "casual" games have noted (Cassell and Jenkins 1998), this usually marks a rough gender divide: women constitute a significant proportion of online game players, but the games that they play the most tend to be discounted by the (mostly male) gaming media, developers, and others as "simple" (or "casual") games, and therefore their players are not "gamers." An example is Scrabulous, a version of Scrabble that in 2008 was very popular on the networking site Facebook. Often these games are marked by a significant social component—they provide a context for game playing and other social interaction. I would also suggest that such games rely more on stochastic elements (which are loosely tied to games labeled as more "luck"-based than "skill"-based). For Linden Lab, at least part of the test of the legitimacy of game-derived outcomes is that the game is not a "social" game but rather an individual one, even if it is one which many people happen to play, and that furthermore it is a game that can be pointed to as emphasizing performative competence over chance.

This is consistent with what we recall from the early imaginings and then versions of Second Life, about which Rosedale reported some surprise that Second Life was generating secondary, social effects. Repeatedly in my discussions with Lindens, but most often with some of the developers, I was brought up short by the realization that they had not expected the cultural aspects of Second Life to happen at all, and they were still very much in a period of adjustment in this regard. For

Lindens within the company, the same assumption held true. One can see the emphasis on Lindens as primarily individuals exercising enlightened judgment in one of the sections from the "Tao of Linden" (reprinted in appendix A):

Your Choice Is Your Responsibility
There's a dual meaning here.

Most companies tell you what to do. Then they make you accountable to the person who told you what to do, not to yourself. We don't think this gets the best long-term results with a truly ambitious project like Second Life. At Linden Lab, you are expected to choose your own work, you have to decide how you can best move the company forward. This isn't always easy, but it can be very rewarding for you and it is a huge win for the company. This doesn't mean that you can't ask someone else what to do   it means that you are responsible for choosing who to listen to! You are responsible for listening well and broadly enough to choose wisely.

And once you have chosen, you are responsible for executing well to [make] your choices work. You must understand that other people now rely on you for single-minded execution, and it is time to shut out the noise and work without distraction. Sometimes you will fail, and in those cases it is very important to fail fast and fail publicly—that is how we learn and iterate and ultimately win.

This document neatly fits together the gaming metaphor with notions of individual choice and individual performance. Failures are legitimate (and public). The "huge win" is the emergent effect of all these individual choices, themselves made in the context of an open-ended system and without social "noise."

Not Quite Content

We again encounter the (initially) unexpected intrusion of the social when we revisit Tringo as the most popular game in Second Life, but first we are presented with a puzzle of our own. While I have suggested the increasing significance of a distinction between game players and game makers, the content tools that Linden Lab provides in Second Life seem to suggest that Linden Lab did not only imagine its users as gamers, but as makers (*Homo fabricans*, perhaps). They provide their users with a gamelike interface to an interactive and persistent environment with a built-in physics, but they also provide a set of tools for making in that environment, and the marketing emphasis throughout much of 2005 was on making. For Boellstorff, this effort underwrote the "creationist capitalism" which characterizes Second Life. As he writes: "In creationist capitalism, the prosumer has become a kind of minor god, and we find not predestination but a performative notion of production that assumes the relationship between the economic and the social is [complicit]. . . . In creationist capitalism it is persons who create, not God" (2008: 209). This picture neatly skips over how this creation may be better understood as acts of *making* within a system that others (certain Lindens) are *creating*. "Making," in this view, sits precariously between "gaming" and "creating." In acts of making within Second Life were its users seen by Lindens as more like gamers or more like creators? To answer this question, it helps to examine the content creation tools provided to Second Life users more closely.

As I have noted, this set of tools also owes a great deal to games, but not to what game players typically experience. Instead, it owes a lot to what some game *developers* do (often called "content developers"). Three-dimensional modeling, scripting (programming), and texture mapping are the tools with which content developers make the "stuff" that fills a computer game: the items, the buildings, the avatars, the trees. This is interesting to consider in the broader sense of the nature of creativity as imagined by Linden Lab in its initial design. Charged with creating an environment for "making," in a limitless sense, what tools did the early Lindens feel were the foundational ones necessary for this grand purpose? The very same ones used by content teams in computer game companies everywhere. "Content" as originally conceived around Linden Lab was boundless in ambition but quite narrow and bound to a specific notion of making. As one developer put it, "We don't have to hire five thousand people to make and build content for us, they're all doing it all and they're paying us."

Because of this, some of the innovative uses of Second Life were a challenge for Linden Lab to grasp, and this was revealed in the changing status of "content" around Linden Lab. Even in 2005, it was clear that for the most part Second Life "content" was for Lindens content in the game developer sense: stuff that was built, scripted, and texture-mapped in Second Life. As users created other things, such as support groups, or social events, Lindens had to work to get in the habit of thinking of these social creations—which depended little if at all on the conventional content creation tools—as content just the same (see Malaby 2006c for a more complete discussion of this issue). This also has implications for the status of creativity around Linden Lab: the original tools for content creation in Second Life at least suggest a view that game content tools are all someone needs to make, well, anything.

But the content creation tools, even though they include a programming language, are not the tools by which the world's foundations (such as the physics engine) themselves are made. Again we see a contrast between creating an environment and making within an environment. By teasing this out a bit more, we can start to see how games influenced how Lindens imagined themselves and their users in these two distinct ways—as game makers and as game players. The easiest way to do this is to consider again the example of Tringo.

Given the gaming background of many company employees, there was a continuing interest around Linden Lab in making Second Life appeal to gamers. But there was significant tension in 2005 because Second Life in fact did *not* appeal to gamers, or at least not as much as many at Linden Lab would have wanted. Around the time that Tringo was beginning to make a splash (the first quarter of 2005), I noticed something a bit surprising: Tringo was *not* the focus of Linden talk about what would lead to an influx of new residents. Another effort to make an in-world game preoccupied and involved Linden Lab, and that was a project called Chinatown (or more properly, U:SL—Chinatown). Whereas Kermitt Quirk, the maker of Tringo, worked on his own and to a certain extent below the radar, a development team of residents within Second Life was working to build an elaborate FPS game on an island in Second Life.

This team, Bedazzle, involved a number of well-known builders, scripters, and mappers and was run by a user with a strong reputation as a project manager, as demonstrated in several of Bedazzle's prior projects. Chinatown was to be the culmination of Second Life's technical capabilities, at least as a gamer might measure them: an actual real-time FPS, with its own homemade combat system, multiple weapons, fast and responsive action, and a gorgeously rendered environment—a few blocks of a mythical "Chinatown"—in which to play. It was also to be a culmination of Second Life's promise as an environment for creativity, especially creativity that was collaborative. Chinatown would testify to the world's viability as a *development environment*, one in which a globally far-flung team could coordinate and produce a sophisticated product (see figure 3).

Before its opening, Chinatown was featured on the Second Life home page, and the office was abuzz with excitement about it. Again, for a company with many employees with backgrounds in computer games, who loved to play Tribes at the end of the day, this anticipation was understandable. This was content in the gaming sense, this was what Second Life could do, and this would bring in at least a portion of the potentially huge audience of gamers and game developers out there. Tringo, meanwhile, continued to grow, and one heard it mentioned around the office as something fun and worth checking out. By February 2005 roughly one in four in-world events was a Tringo competition—a staggering number. Tringo's success and subsequent licensing shouldered the highly touted Chinatown project aside. Chinatown itself, while widely lauded for the beauty of its design, suffered from serious lag problems, especially the more users played it. Second Life is always a moving target for Linden Lab's marketing team, and they deftly shifted gears to promote Tringo more prominently.

But the Tringo/Chinatown example should direct us to a striking insight into how Linden Lab tended to imagine its users. In seeking to make an environment for game making, Linden Lab was drawing the

Figure 3. A promotional screenshot for Bedazzle's game USL: Chinatown, depicting a scene from the few blocks of a mythical Chinatown located on an island in Second Life.

division between game makers and game players at a different point from the one we might expect. Chinatown was supposed to be the culmination of what Second Life could do because it would testify to a productive relationship between the makers of an environment (Linden Lab) and the makers of games within that environment. By providing the tools with which to make games like Chinatown within Second Life, Linden Lab did only *part* of what a game developer might do—it created the fundamental parameters for further work as well tools to do that work. The "content" work would be done by a different group, the users, in a wholly different relationship to their environment. Their tools were not for tinkering "under the hood," as Lindens put it.

In drawing the distinction between game makers and world creators in this way, Linden Lab was recreating a broader trend in the gaming industry, in which a developer (Id, Epic, Havok, to name a few) provides a "game engine," which includes the physics engine and other tools for game development, but no game "content" to other developers. These developers pay to license these engines (some are freely available as well), and then, much like Second Life users, create the content to go into them to make a complete game. So what was going on here? Linden Lab, by providing the fundamental conditions of Second Life, was offering, in a sense, a ready-made game engine with built-in tools for game content developers. The added value, from their point of view, was that Second Life is theoretically accessible from anywhere in the world with a broadband Internet connection. The Bedazzle team had members in several different countries, many of whom never met face-to-face. Chinatown was supposed to show that Second Life was a gaming "platform," as it was called around Linden Lab.

Nonetheless, the surprising success of Tringo over Chinatown was not a refutation of this point of view for Lindens. For themselves as well as for Second Life, Lindens on the whole saw complex processes engaged by individuals pursuing enlightened self-interest as the legitimate path to self-governance; that is, to emergent effects that would be right by virtue of that emergence. Second Life was supposed to govern itself in this way, assuming that "access to tools" was ensured. Tringo's surprising rise and the way it pushed Chinatown out of the Linden Lab marketing spotlight was, despite the way it ran contrary to many Lindens' expectations, a proof for Linden Lab of just this logic. This was because, at a "meta" level, the broader game of Second Life had led to an unforeseen outcome: Tringo had trumped Chinatown for Second Life users.

For Linden Lab, the fact that their environment had spawned such divergent attempts at game making and the unexpected "win" by Tringo was something that confirmed their approach—they had successfully contrived contingency. Even game making was a game in Second Life, and this competition and outcome testified to Second Life as a well-made game itself. This helps us understand the continuing categorical confusion of Second Life. Was it a game, or was it not a game? In a way, we might say that Second Life was something like a game engine—it contained many of the elements of games but depended on the further making of content by users to exhibit the indeterminate outcomes that games generate. The outcome, in this case, was legitimate, even though contrary to many Lindens' expectations. The broader lesson that they might have taken from Tringo's success—that of the importance of the "casual," the random, and the social over individual mastery—was not explicitly confronted. Like the many ways in which the social seemed to surprise Linden Lab, Tringo's success was taken as a surprising testament to the world's robustness, but not as an illuminating critique of their own imagining of the human.

For the Elo ranking of Jira tasks, we can see a similar distinction between game players and game makers at work. Access to the game provides an opportunity for agency on the part of its players, who collectively contribute to an emergent outcome. The Linden who was the game creator set the conditions of the game implicitly, however, and resided in its unfolding to a great extent behind the scenes. The plausibility of this as a strategy for generating a basis for decisions at Linden Lab was never questioned publicly (although misgivings about it were voiced to me privately). This did not keep the outcomes of the game from being *practically* illegitimate, however. The ranking did not ring true enough for either a sufficient number of Lindens as a whole or those Lindens at the top of the organization to point to it as a basis for what should be done next. Instead, there were further refinements of voting for Jira tasks (including more prominently rewarding those who had completed tasks that had received more votes).

As we move forward with an understanding of the nature of virtual worlds as domains for human action, we must pay close attention to the relationship among political ideals, professional practice, and the allure of games as instruments of social policy. Future work will be essential for ferreting out the new place of games and gaming practice in our political and digital lives to come. The emerging social distinctions between system (or world) creators, game makers, and game players constitute an important thread in the currently expanding digital society. The techniques of game design give institutions tools for contriving open-endedness, and they are then always applied with particular ideas about the human in mind. In this case, an imagining of the gamer as an individual performing within a complex system underwrote both the kinds of games that Lindens tried to use to sort out their own self-governance and the kinds of games whose success they imagined would constitute proof of Second Life's viability.[13]

4_THE BIRTH OF THE COOL

I received my eye-in-hand pendant, attached to a thin, black leather cord, during a visit to Linden Lab in the late spring of 2005. It is, in essence, the logo for Second Life turned into a wearable symbol of connection to Second Life. I had already noticed the pendants around the office—Rosedale was always wearing his, and I counted thirteen visible out of thirty-eight present employees during a trip I made in June. They have a hand-wrought quality, with the symbol—set in relief over a rough gray background—shiny and polished as though from long natural wear (see figure 4). One of the Lindens gave me mine; I detected a slightly amused gleam in her eye as she gave it to me. For the anthropologist in me, to be given such an item prompted a cavalcade of associations (about reciprocity, symbols, and more), but I think there is a danger of reading too much into such things, so I will resist the temptation here. But I certainly was left with the feeling, on every return visit, that at least a few Lindens were on the lookout to see if I had started to wear mine. I never did, but I appreciated the gesture.

What immediately caught my attention was not the pendant, but the accompanying text, printed on a small card that also bore the Second Life logo and Web site address: "The eye observes the world, the hand

Figure 4. A Second Life pendant, given to me by Linden Lab after several visits for research. The text of the accompanying card invokes creativity and Second Life.

shapes it. For this reason, many cultures embrace the eye-in-hand as a symbol of creation that springs from knowledge—as do we. Take it as your invitation to help create a Second Life that inspires ever more wonder, ever more imagination." I do not know for certain the origin of the text, but it was symptomatic of the twin ideas of creation and creativity as they circulated around Linden Lab in 2005. "Creativity" (later "collaborative creativity") was one of the signal values that Second Life was designed to promote. It was equally important for the employees of Linden Lab. Prospective employees were explicitly judged in terms of their creativity, intelligence, and energy. The concept also clearly underlies the distinction between the makers of content (*Homo fabricans*) and the makers of the world (*Homo creans*) and in doing so further reflects an idea about what constitutes creation, in this case with implications for governance and authority. The focus in both cases is on the individual, either making through action within a system (and to be nudged away from social effects) or creating the system as a whole (including the ongoing tweaking of that system after its genesis).[1]

When we think about the act of creation through technology, one illuminating analogy can be found in the work of the historian of science and technology Jessica Riskin (2003), who has written about the "automata" of the eighteenth century. Automata were mechanical devices (they included a woman harpsichordist and a paddling swan) that sought not just to mimic the behaviors of living things (that is, simply in outward appearance) but to simulate the processes of living things, internal and external. One of the most famous of these was Vaucanson's "defecating duck," a mechanical duck that consumed grain and then seemed to evacuate it, digested. Riskin argues that the origins of current artificial life efforts are to be found in these early attempts, which already showed the tension between the simulation of life processes via mechanics and their merely external imitation. All such efforts, she suggests, had to mask the limits of the maker's ability to achieve simulation, and shortcuts or other compromises were a potential source of scandal. Vaucanson's duck was "strictly simulative, except where it was not" (Riskin 2003: 609), and the fact that the product of its "eating" was not in fact the same substance, transformed, but a different one (which had to be preloaded into the machine) was a black mark. Similarly, Stefan Helmreich (1998) in his study of the Santa Fe Institute, a center for artificial life research, found that the success of the institute's efforts to "culture" artificial life continued to depend on the ability to simulate certain aspects of life, and not others. The imperfections of the endeavors were disregarded so that attention could be drawn to the similarities, and in this striking commonality lay a certain promise of humankind's ability to recreate the world (and thereby be seen as able to conquer it).

Second Life, despite the name, is not exactly an artificial life project, because it does not seek to create life sui generis (that is, it is based on participation by people). But nonetheless some of the parallels are instructive. In its user interface and elsewhere one's "second life" is held up as on a par with one's "first life," and there is little doubt that Second Life depends as much upon its analogous relationship to the affordances of first life (the avatar/body, the familiar, gravity-simulating physics) as it does to new capabilities (such as flight). In an official Second Life blog post titled, "The Mission of Linden Lab" Rosedale invoked simulation explicitly (see appendix B):

My best definition of our mission is that we are working to create an online world having the exceptional property that it advances the capabilities of the many people that use it, and by doing so affects and transforms them in a positive way. More specifically, since there are so many possible definitions of "online world," we are trying to create a close reproduction of the actual physical world we live in— one that will be easily comprehensible and useful to us because it will so closely resemble ours. The ability to simulate our world on computers means that we can make it different in ways that empower us, allowing us to do things that in the physical world we can imagine but are incapable of.

Again we can see two "levels" of creation here. At its most basic level, the world of Second Life is a created world, and in its affordances it is supposed to simulate our first life, except where it does not. In contrast to Vaucanson's duck, however, here Second Life's departures from pure simulation are not failures to be masked but rather intentional enhancements. They are held to be in all cases consciously designed and thereby able to serve the public good through the expansion of individual expressive creativity ("we can make it different in ways that empower us"). So designed, at this second level, Second Life stands as a place where next-order creation (creation within the system) takes place, and where simulation of offline experience allows for all the familiar capabilities of life offline, as well as the designed broadening of those capabilities for the greater good of all.

The tension between the goal of absolute simulation and the ability to create improvements was recognizable in certain debates at Linden Lab. One, just before I completed my research in early 2006, concerned whether users should be allowed to customize their daylight/nighttime settings. A Linden put the core issues succinctly in an e-mail:

There are two opposing motivations: (1) We are a tool, a platform. We are plastic: users mold us as they feel. They should be able to put the damn sun wherever they want. (2) We are a simulation of the real world. Things happen naturally, and the residents build their lives

around universal truths and natural cycles. We build by day and we
party by night. Trying to satisfy both of these motivations is the
problem, I think.

Simulation implies a commitment to a certain kind of *constraint*—to
the idea that by faithfully reproducing something (such as the conditions of offline life) you will support creative activity. But the metaphor
of the tool suggests a readiness to change conditions when called for to
support local interests or desires. As with the telehubs, the difficulty is
one of public policy—it is possible that to some extent Second Life's
users might not, in fact, know what is good for them. On the whole, in
these kind of arguments, holding to a position that governance of Second Life must run against individual user preferences was a difficult
argument to sustain, because it contradicted the ideals of trusting aggregate individual decision making and open access (participation).
Nonetheless, in *practice* the largely implicit distinction between world
makers and world users that shaped attitudes around Linden Lab allowed just enough momentum for Linden Lab to retain ultimate control over what was "under the hood."

All this is important for understanding the nature of creativity
around Linden Lab, and furthermore how creativity influenced other
kinds of notions and practices there. The "cool," for example, was another trope that, like game and tools, could be invoked to solve the
continuing puzzle of what to do next. It was an appeal to an aesthetic
claim, one that suggested that something (a feature, a tool) carried
with it the promise of future creative use, use that could not be further
specified in the moment at hand. Creativity also informed the practice
of "secret projects" around Linden Lab. These were projects that employees were encouraged to initiate and work on in secret, in notable
and illuminating tension with Linden Lab's stated ideal of transparency (see appendix A). Such a project might fail—privately—but it also
might issue forth in the ultimate creative act around Linden Lab, the
"proof of concept," where a demonstration of a creation stands itself as
testament to its viability as a solution to a recognized problem or dilemma. When Lindens sought to assess creativity in their potential

employees, it was also informed by these ideas and practices. As a result, while all Lindens who were hired were, almost by definition, equally creative, some were more creative than others.

For Second Life, as well, Linden Lab has been invested in creativity through its need to support the content creation of its users, and the tools of the world reflect an emphasis on content creation of a particular sort. While all this was happening, however—while more powerful scripting and building tools were added, and while selling its content outside the world itself began to expand—more and more users within Second Life joined and began to engage the world *without* building, scripting, or texture mapping. One of the most notable developments in this regard was the result of a secret project and the feature it brought to Second Life.

Dance Dance Revolution

The new development followed the release of version 1.4. This version, like most releases, included new capabilities for users. Linden Lab had worked hard to include avatar animations in 1.4, the ability to write script that would animate your avatar performing an activity. According to recollections of those working at Linden Lab at the time, there was a great deal of Linden anticipation about this new capability, and the staff expected to see users scripting a wide variety of animations for everyday activities (smoking a cigarette, leaning casually, etc.). Shortly before release, a Linden unveiled, in a proof of concept demo, the result of his project—the ability to stream audio content (music) from a user's computer into Second Life (for example, onto land that the user owned). Other users visiting the land would then hear it as well. Linden Lab realized that they could also easily add ("throw in") this capability, which seemed "cool" but was not expected to have a huge impact on Second Life. What happened next was a remarkable and entirely unanticipated in-world phenomenon entirely dependent on these two features combined: dance clubs. Users built dance floors, sometimes just on bare land, sometimes amid huge structures, and streamed dance music from their PCs, while other users scripted avatar animations in the form of dances. They then sold these animations to users (or clubs, which made them available for free).

Dance clubs continue to be a significant part of Second Life social activity and have taken their place in Linden Lab's marketing efforts for the world, but as an example of creativity they posed a challenge to prevailing expectations at Linden Lab. What kind of content were the dance clubs, and what kind of creativity did they signal? They involved little to no technical skill to create, either in scripting or texture mapping, but by late 2004 they were by far the most popular in-world places, and they continued through 2005 to vie with Tringo as the most popular sites for interaction.

Dance clubs contributed to the recognition of a new kind of resident for Linden Lab, one who, by some off-the-cuff estimates, may account for up to 80 percent of the users: consumers. These are users who do not make their own content and instead are happy to purchase objects, avatars, skins, accessories, animations, and the like. It is these users who helped bring about the boom in Second Life's economy throughout the latter half of 2005, and they turned much of Second Life into a commodified landscape. Linden Lab began to make a transition from appealing to content creators to appealing to consumers.

In this transition the marketing team led the way. Marketing was generally held to be in tension with development in Linden Lab (and, Lindens said, at software companies generally), and this was marked most strongly by consistently different claims about authority. While the developers, as a whole, reflected the technoliberal attitude I have outlined, Lindens in marketing regularly reported a preference for more vertical control and direction. In similar ways, their imagining of potential Second Life users was shaped less by the ideal of individual creative self-expression through actual object creation and instead fit quite well a modern consumerist ideal of individual self-expression through consumption. When Tringo surpassed Chinatown, and when dance clubs (and fashion) took over Second Life, the marketing team was able to respond with campaigns that played to these more broadly established ideals. An online ad created in Spring 2005 (a parody of an ad by the Gap that had appeared earlier that season) speaks to this effort (the illustration can be found at www.uwm.edu/~malaby/SLAP image.gif).

In this ad the marketing team at Linden Lab identified users who had created striking custom avatars (a form of content creation that emphasizes texture mapping) and inserted them into a clickable ad that poked fun at the Gap's pretensions while pointing to the possibilities and distinctiveness of Second Life as a comparable world. The text of the ad, which in every phrase was a slightly altered version of Gap's original ad copy, is revealing: "enjoy being whatever you want in Second Life"; "there's more at secondlife.com. more avatars. more fashion. more possibility." The marketing imperative to reach an audience of potential users pushed one aspect of the values that, in Linden Lab's view, characterize Second Life—its limitless possibility—into the realm of marketing discourse, as the ad makes an explicit link between the contingency of the world and individual freedom of expression. The appeal of Second Life, in this presentation, rests in its potential as a place where you, the user, can express your uniqueness, your individuality, and be unlike anyone else, including your "real life" self. The New Communalist ideal of individualized expressive creativity through broad access to technology (tools) is self-evident here, but there is an instructive ambiguity in the simultaneous highlighting of unique Second Life creators along with the suggestion that similar distinctiveness can be achieved simply through consumption.

Given the reduced content creators' "overhead" in making these commodities, their competition for Second Life users' Linden dollars is over design, and fashion rules much of the market in Second Life. Potential new users are told that they can "enjoy being whatever they want in Second Life," but for most of them this seems to involve buying clothes and other items that thousands of others have bought as well. The consumers of Second Life seem largely untroubled by their lack of technical engagement with the world's tools, although a vocal minority have at times raised concerns that, in comparison with content creators, they feel ignored by Linden Lab. But Linden Lab's ability to serve these two kinds of users sprang forth from their own internal tensions, the multiple ways in which they imagined users. While the ideal of content creation continued to be deeply inscribed in the world's tools and its continuing new features, consumerism was not neglected. It was supported not only in marketing materials but in the support for the world's economy itself, in particular the ability to exchange national currencies for Linden dollars. In fact, Linden Lab's taking over of this exchange, primarily from a user-created company, Gaming Open Market (GOM), that had pioneered the ability to buy Linden dollars via credit card was one of their most controversial moves, as it showed Linden Lab's willingness to claim a kind of "eminent domain" over areas they claimed were essential to their business interests (even when users had innovated in these areas). This move continues to haunt Second Life, as Boellstorff (2008) notes that in Second Life to be "gommed" means to have one's creation co-opted by Linden Lab.

Consumerism is an inescapable value written into Second Life at a broader level. We need only note how a core attribute of Second Life, its granting of intellectual property rights to all users over what they make, so easily serves both the ideal of empowered creation and the ideal of consumption. Developers in Linden Lab were more likely to grumble about the latter. One groused to me about the rise of land barons (owners of vast amounts of in-world land, who then developed and rented it) as precisely why Second Life was heading in the wrong direction: "Why should people who don't *make* anything in Second Life be the richest users?")

Across these developments one sees a common trend—content seems in Second Life particularly vulnerable to commodification, and the emerging distinction between content creators and consumers seems to stand in rather marked contrast to the exaltation of collaborative, technically skilled creativity that underwrites Second Life's public face. Consumers are nonetheless obviously a boon to Second Life, and this was recognized around Linden Lab. Their purchasing of stuff (made possible because they bought Linden dollars through Linden Lab) is the ongoing engine of Second Life's economy. But there was little readiness to see this kind of action by users in Second Life as "creative" around Linden Lab, and there is a parallel here to a class of

Linden Lab employee activity that, while also essential and ongoing, could not qualify as creative. This speaks to the parallel range of jobs at Linden Lab and how they were viewed on a mostly unspoken scale from very creative to not creative at all and the ways employees felt they were judged based on their place in this classification system.

Projects and Proof

At the creative end of the scale were the "secret projects." The chess ranking system for Jira was a kind of secret project, though on a smaller scale than they were typically characterized (usually secret projects were discussed as if they would take weeks, rather than days). Another such effort was the "Silver Bells and Golden Spurs" (SBGS) project by one of Linden Lab's content team. SBGS was a machinima project. Machinima can be described as a new kind of filmmaking that is produced within virtual worlds. Game-based virtual world makers have seen an explosion of machinima produced by their players that make use of their worlds (at the time of this writing, machinima-based videos are common on YouTube). Most game makers, such as Blizzard (makers of World of Warcraft) and Microsoft (makers of Halo), have sought to capitalize on this user-generated content by sponsoring contests, featuring popular machinima on their Web sites, and the like. For Linden Lab, this kind of use of Second Life was to be encouraged. There were, however, initial challenges that had led to a prevailing skepticism about Second Life's viability as a machinima "platform," such as the limits on "camera" use when every camera was effectively an avatar (and thus constrained by that avatar's physics in the world).

The Linden who began SBGS saw his project as a way to counter this opinion practically. As he put it in an online publication about his experience, available through Second Life's official Web site (Call 2005: 3, emphasis added),

> As an exploration of the movie making capabilities of Second Life, and as a *proof of concept* for doing such, I chose to produce a short

western film based on an old poem called "Silver Bells and Golden Spurs."

The functionality of Second Life as a movie making medium turned a corner with the release of v1.4, which provided its residents the ability to create custom avatar animations and upload them in world.

Although still in development, the power and diversity of Second Life as a platform for movie making is obvious. As improvements are made to support and simplify the processes used for modeling, texturing, animation, and video capture, residents in Second Life will find this environment perfect for telling stories through film.

With all the available tools in Second Life, including customized art and animation, as well as the collaboration of other residents, anyone can create beautiful, compelling movies only limited by his or her imagination.

Like the lighting demonstration I observed in my first months at Linden Lab, this effort was a good example of the kind of project that counted as creative in one sense and demonstrates how the notion of a "proof of concept" stands as a practical (rather than discursive) means by which an argument can be made. The best way to convince people that something can be done, proofs of concept suggest, is simply to do it, if only in a rough and unpolished fashion. The proof of concept for SBGS was not the full-length film but a brief snippet of a scene produced by Call, without dialogue and other features.

All employees at Linden Lab were told at one point (I could not determine precisely when, but some Lindens recalled it as early 2004) that they were free to pursue "secret projects." They could devote up to 20 percent of their time to such a project (that is, one working day a week). What were such projects, and why were they secret? The idea, as a number of Lindens consistently described it to me, was that employees should have the freedom to pursue an idea that might or might not bear fruit. That is, the idea was held up as a way to legitimize the pursuit of ideas that might fail (and this connects as well to an oft-heard mantra around Linden Lab, the misquoted Maoist statement

"Let a thousand flowers bloom").[2] Someone might have an idea about how to incorporate an Internet chat client into Second Life or how to stream audio from users' computers into Second Life (as described above).

The secrecy of the projects was essential, under this reasoning, because a dead end, discovered only after weeks of work, could remain that Linden's secret. There is an irony here, however, given the strong emphasis on transparency as a value around Linden Lab. The broad dissemination of information was not only preferred to improve the productivity of the company but was in fact held up as a moral issue. In the "Tao of Linden" we can see it appear several times, but most obviously in the section "Be Transparent and Open" (see appendix A):

> There are many ways to emphasize responsibility, accountability, communication, and trust. We believe that the one key principle that best supports all of these values is transparency. As much as possible, tell everyone what you are doing, all the time. This transparency makes us responsible to our peers, makes us accountable to our own statements, and replaces the need for management with individual responsibility. Over time, it creates and reinforces trust. Be willing to share ideas before you feel they are "baked." Report on your own progress frequently and to everyone.

Public failure, too, is valorized as essential to the company's goals, as in the quote from the "Your Choice Is Your Responsibility" section that I introduced in the previous chapter: "Sometimes you will fail, and in those cases it is very important to fail fast and fail publicly—that is how we learn and iterate and ultimately win."

The expressed importance of *not* being transparent about secret projects seemed not to raise a contradiction in my discussions with Lindens, although I got the sense that the secret projects were not widely pursued around the company:

> It was sort of launched at one point a long time ago . . . a year and a half ago, something like that. It seems like a long time anyway. And

I think there was a lot of buy-in for a while. . . . I think Karl and Max have always been really big believers . . . Karl, because he is a broad thinker. He wants to impact the company on every level I think at some point. . . . But he's quiet, so I think for him these secret projects are a way for him to be noisier and more opinionated—by doing things that he thinks are accomplishing those goals.

Projects were in this sense a practical way to be "opinionated," and stand as a nondiscursive means to make an argument about what the company should do next. Little more is to be said about the contradiction between transparency and secret projects—it was discursively overlooked, and therefore any given practice could be supported or criticized in relation to these opposing values.

The primary stage for a proof of concept demo was a Friday lunch, when the result could be unveiled. I saw a few of these during my Fridays at Linden Lab, including the demo for SBGS, an Second Life database searchable from outside Second Life, and a proposed new login animation. Such meetings always involved, after the initial presentation, a question and answer period, where the potential of the new feature or capability could be roughly assessed. It was in such conversations that an appeal to the cool would most likely be heard ("Let's add that to the next release—it's really cool"). The idea of adding Web browsing to Second Life belonged, in the words of one developer to the category of "stuff we think is nifty"—no one had really requested it, and people at Linden Lab could not say exactly what its usefulness would be, but still it merited this positive aesthetic label. Such possible features suggested a range of possibilities, impossible to identify ahead of time. The coolest tools were those that skated on the edge of their own obvious utility, leading directly to an immediate set of guesses as to possible use but, more important, describing an arc of further yet unspecified improvisations. In the absence of an evidence-based argument in their favor, an aesthetic appeal rises to prominence as a way to push for these additions.

Of course, it bears mentioning that it can matter *who* labels something cool—such an assessment from Rosedale or Ondrejka carried a great deal of weight (cultural capital in the form of credentials; see also Bourdieu's discussion of the "skeptron"; 1999: 107–116). The importance of possibly catching Rosedale's attention and therefore his support with a "cool" idea was widely noted to me in private interviews, although it was not a topic publicly acknowledged. One Linden put it to me as follows, "Philip will get very excited about something without really seeing it through to its logical end." Another Linden was more concise, if nonetheless willing to exaggerate for comic effect: "For Philip, it's, 'Look, something shiny!'" The company's forward orientation, toward an uncertain future, grounded their guesswork in such aesthetic appeals, supplementing the other appeals to tools and to games that I have already explored.

I suggest, however, that the kinds of projects Lindens pursued in this way were not all candidates for the cool label in this grand sense. The most important thing to notice is that not every project aimed at making and providing a new tool to Second Life. The question was whether a project "moved the company forward" (a phrase found not only in the two documents by Rosedale reprinted in the appendices, but which also appeared regularly in e-mails from him). This was part of a general commitment to *progress* that one could find in many of the company's documents and as a part of their practices of evaluating each other's work (as at Friday lunch demos). The most explicit statement is, again, from the "Tao of Linden," in the "Make Weekly Progress" section:

We believe that every person should make specific, visible individual contributions that moves [sic] the company forward every week. Projects must be broken down into measurable tasks so that making weekly progress is possible. This is a principle that almost no one believes is true when they first hear it, yet everyone who keeps to this principle over the course of several months is stunned by the amount of progress made during that time. Set weekly goals and report progress to everyone. Regardless how big what you are working on may be, you can always break it down this way. Give it a try.

This idea of progress is consonant with the attitude toward technology that suffuses Linden Lab. Tools, for example, allow one to go about the work of making or crafting, and access to the right tools allows for, it seems, more efficient pursuit of these ends (with lasting and positive aggregate consequences, goes the logic). The proof of concept demo scene for SBGB, for example, was not only to prove that movies could be made in Second Life but also to argue for what tools were still needed to make such creation easier (such as camera control tools, or lip synchronization tools). Did making that demo scene "move the company forward" in other Lindens' eyes? Probably, given the largely positive response to it, but other acts of creation were less likely to be given such credit.

In July 2005 I was sitting at an outdoor café, with a view of San Francisco Bay and the numerous piers along the Embarcadero, with another Linden, one who worked in a part of the company that was regularly presented with so-called "recurring" tasks (I will avoid even a gender identification in what follows to further protect identity). This Linden pointed out that, on arriving at Linden Lab, it was made very clear that recurring tasks should not be included in As & Os, and the Linden went on to note, with a wry smile, that "As & Os wouldn't be very useful to a janitor, for example," someone whose day is filled with recurring tasks. About the Linden's own As & Os, the quip was pointed: "Mine tend to be quite short." This quickly led to a discussion of time, recurring tasks, and creativity. It was not just that the Linden's job happened to be one that involved a lot of recurring tasks. The point was that, by occupying that kind of position in this kind of company, where such tasks were generally not valued, this Linden's time was further filled by this kind of work—it was not as if, the Linden pointed out, the Linden could attract other people to the project. In fact, this work did not really *exist* as a project (in the As & Os, or Jira, sense). The contrast, the Linden continued, was "to developers, who are always solving unique problems."

But even this local assessment of the distinction bears some inspection. In what sense were the tasks of this Linden not unique? Or, to put it another way, in what sense were they "recurring"? All "infrastructural" tasks at Linden Lab had a kind of uniqueness, from moment to moment. A sysadmin, working to keep the "back-end" servers running for Second Life, the company Web site, or the internal network had to confront somewhat patterned kinds of breakdowns but also unique problems that demanded urgent and creative attention. Things could always break in new ways. Similarly, those handling "abuse reports" (complaints filed by users against other users) had, in one sense, a never-ending queue before them, one for which no end condition was possible. But every call was different in one way or another, demanding of the Linden a new angle, phrase, or moderation of tone to deal with an emotionally charged situation and move forward. In light of this reality, it seems difficult to sustain a conviction that such work was not creative.

If developers' projects were in some sense paradigmatic of creativity, what were the characteristics that distinguished them from this "recurring" work? To start with, work that "move[d] the company forward" was work that could be completed. As Rosedale wrote in an e-mail about Jira, "Tasks, Bugs, and Projects should always result in clear forward progress for LL [Linden Lab] if completed." But it is not simply the possibility of completion that defined a creative task around Linden Lab, because acute system administration problems had clear "work complete" conditions (server back up or its firmware updated, etc.). Such tasks *were* able to appear in As & Os (emergency tasks could appear under the "bonus" category), but they did not appear in Jira. This was not because they were disallowed, but because it made little sense to take the several minutes to create a Jira task for often extremely urgent problems. Jira tasks, generally speaking, had a specific time horizon. They took long enough that it made some sense to create a Jira task for them but not so long as to be impossible to finish (or, impossible to divide into completable subtasks). So Jira excluded at least three types of tasks: those that had no clear end conditions, those that recurred again and again (under some implicit portrayal of how similar each instance was), and those that were so pressing that to involve Jira would be counterproductive.

To push this further, however, we can recall how tools "flowed" *within* Linden Lab. To get work done, Lindens relied on software, and much of it was coded by other employees (developers) of Linden Lab. This was a source of ongoing tension, as nondevelopers often found themselves beholden to the interests and schedules of developers and at times felt that they were not as involved in the creation of the tool as they could have been, with less than ideal results. A Linden on the content team spoke directly to the issue in an interview when I asked what was the primary challenge he had in working with other Lindens (which he took to mean developers):

> Giving us the right tools. The issue that I had with them just jumping in and developing tools is, since I'm a person who uses those all day long, it just seems logical to me that you would want to inquire, "What do you need?" You know, "What works, what doesn't work, what needs improvement?" Subsequently we as a team have had to wrangle a few engineers and in the course of a couple of big meetings say, "we have to have this, we have to have this," and really just put our foot down. And I hate to do that, because they don't like it. . . . [T]hat upsets their apple cart a little bit, and I understand that, but that would be overcome if there was more dialogue before the work began. It's like I say, they would jump in and do a project and create something that we would see immediate benefit [from], but it's not necessarily the right benefit, you know what I mean?

The broader point is that not only was there a generally acknowledged (if problematic) distinction between recurring work and creative tasks, but there was also a distinction between kinds of creative tasks. In making SBGS, for example, Call could show that Second Life was a viable machinima platform, but it was also one more way to argue that some developer time should be devoted to coding the tools to make it easier—those tools, and by extension not others.

SBGS itself stands in contrast to other kinds of content creation done by Lindens as part of the time they spent on special projects. Linden Lab's marketing team often organized in-world events in conjunction with a "first life" conference or the like (such as the Game Developers Conference, or GDC). They would often use a dramatic in-world structure as the location, something that might be used only once but needed to make a significant impact. They might recreate the offline location in Second Life (a nightclub, for example), so that two parties could happen at the same time (with video from each streaming to the other). They might also create an in-world site unique to Second Life, or modeled after a famous offline structure (such as a historic hotel). When Lindens (often not from the marketing team) spent time (often many hours) making these builds, there was little sense that the creation merited the kind of credit that SBGS garnered for its maker, to say nothing of the credit that would accrue to someone who created a new tool. The sense that such creations "moved the company forward" was slight or nonexistent.

What does this tell us about the hierarchy of creation that could be found around Linden Lab? First-order creative action within Linden Lab was the ongoing world making that made second-order creative action possible. That is, access to tools to pursue one's own creations depended on their creation by those in a position to do so. While many developers recognized this power imbalance and sought to compensate for it by being on the whole approachable as well as sensitive to the nuances of the requests made of them, the fact remained that they, and only they, could tinker "under the hood" not only of Second Life but also of Linden Lab itself. It is in this sense that both Linden Lab and Second Life were virtual worlds, of a sort. They not only shaped each other through their open-ended and mutually invested trajectories, but they were also to a certain extent contrived through the extensive manipulation of code, and in them we could find the same social distinction between that code's creators and its users.

5_PRECARIOUS AUTHORITY

The distinction I have highlighted between those who contrive a system and those invited to be creative within it marks a number of business efforts in the context of Internet connectivity and the rise of "user-generated content." In 2007 in Second Life, Coca-Cola announced a contest to design an "online 'virtual thirst' Coke machine," a competition aimed primarily at Second Life users and created through the work of two Second Life-located virtual world-marketing companies: Millions of Us and Crayon. As the press release began:

Imagine a vending machine that dispenses entertainment, adventure, or happiness; a device that satisfies curiosities and fulfills virtual wishes.

Coca-Cola is calling on the public to envision and design just such a futuristic appliance. More specifically, The Coca-Cola Company is inviting the virtual community that resides online at Second Life®—or anyone, for that matter, with a view of "the Coke experience of the future"—to submit their most inventive ideas for the next generation of Coke machines.

Michael Donnelly, Coca-Cola's then director of global interactive marketing, is quoted in the release, saying, "There are few restrictions, except that the more inspired and original the idea, the better. This competition is a chance for anyone with a vivid imagination to design an experience that embodies the in-world Coke Side of Life in a way that enhances their lives and the lives of others within Second Life." (As of this writing, a large amount of information about the contest and its winner is available at www.virtualthirst.com.)

The winning entry (The "Lucky Puzzle Bottle" concept) was by Second Life user Anne Marie Mathis (aka Emerie in Second Life) and involved the placing of three large Coke bottles, in pieces, at different locations in Second Life. Each puzzle, when solved, put in place a Coke-themed installation: a snow-globe, complete with penguins, a "bubble ride" inside the large Coke bottle, and a snowball vending machine. The avatar that first reassembled and completed these puzzles was awarded one of three prizes: a Coke-branded scooter, a small polar bear (one of Coca-Cola's long-time motifs) worn on the shoulder, or a Coke-branded guitar. Each of these was then freely copyable and transferable for the winner.

Given the concerns that many existing corporations have about the use of their trademarks and other properties in online communities, this effort by Coca-Cola was hailed as a successful integration of user creativity and a company's marketing, in much the same way as some machinima is sponsored by companies like Blizzard, makers of World of Warcraft. It was furthermore an attempt to reconcile the meaning of a brand associated in part with a particular physical experience (thirst, then "refreshment") with virtual world experiences that, while also involving the body, have little if anything analogous to thirst. At a panel titled "Building Businesses in Virtual Worlds," at a conference on virtual worlds in Singapore, State of Play V (August 19–22, 2007), the virtual thirst campaign was held up as one example of how companies might achieve "sustainable branding," in the words of one of the panelists. The puzzle facing companies in the era of online networking—and the rising expectations of users to be able to create and distribute widely cultural products such as machinima—is how to maintain control over their brands while tapping into the creativity this users' work represents.

Another example, one that further clarifies some of the implications for the emerging divide between makers and creators (as well as illustrating how these are concerns that are not limited to virtual worlds), is the online code-writing contest located at topcoder.com. TopCoder hosts contests (weekly, with a larger one biannually) to code solutions to complex problems. In a manner quite similar to Coca-Cola's efforts, TopCoder owns the code submitted to them in the competitions, paying out a one-time cash award, although "rated" members can join a development team to receive some royalties for commercial uses. In both of these examples we see a number of elements familiar from my account of Linden Lab. Primarily we should notice the turn to game design to encourage participation, specifically the application of effort and cultural capital (competence) to perform in a contrived, indeterminate system. These are not necessarily cases of labor exploitation in the Marxian sense. Further research would be needed to evaluate the nature of this ludo-capitalism, but along with the use of games to attempt to domesticate creativity, we should also notice the implicit distinction here between "players" and the sponsoring institutions that create the conditions for such play.

I am not arguing for a thoroughgoing exploitative account of this relationship between (world/system) creators and (content) makers. To do so would suggest a teleology that I do not intend. No matter the degree of control that Linden Lab, for example, enjoys over Second Life, its control is not complete. The breadth of affordances the company offers users always entails the possibility for contingent outcomes even to the level of disrupting, transforming, or destroying Second Life itself. As I noted before, Linden Lab's willingness to skate on the edge of its and its product's existence by providing such a breadth of affordances was a key element in Second Life's growth and reputation. Instead of providing a heavy-handed critical account, I seek to highlight this social distinction to draw our attention to its emergence around digital technologies, most visibly those offering a broad range of affordances for their users (up to and including virtual worlds). By highlighting the social distinction between creators and makers, I am trying to counteract the prevalence of practical and discursive appeals to individual agency, which itself points to a particular means of imagining games and players. If creativity can be "defined down" to the ability to perform and innovate within a system the architecture of which is largely inaccessible, then an important transformation has occurred, and a great deal of influential creation has been moved offstage. In short, such a development suggests that the successor to the bureaucracies of high modernity are bureaucracies that are contrived to be open-ended, much like games.

This is by no means an easy accommodation, however. Bureaucracies, defined as they are at least by the ideal of constantly ironing out contingency, would in theory find it impossible to incorporate games into their logic in a lasting way. But the issue is not one of theory but one of practice. Whatever opposition games present to bureaucratic logic, that does not keep the people engaged in the work of forging the institutions shaping digital experience from finding practical accommodations between the ultimate institutional aim (the reproduction of the institution itself) and the need to engage human imaginings of possibility. In this, they are in some ways perhaps not so different from those who have always worked in bureaucracies (Herzfeld 1993). What appears to be different now, however, is the explicit institutional acknowledgment of the need to accommodate the indeterminate coupled with a turn to techniques from games to bring this about.

Linden Lab is doing just this kind of work and, to date, has succeeded not only in maintaining its creation but in growing it to a point many at Linden may have hoped for, but via paths that none of them foresaw. There were moments of near-economic collapse, multiple hacker attacks, features added that fell flat, and surprising bursts of participation from the least ballyhooed quarters. Linden Lab had to confront the reality that social uses were a large part of what many of its users found compelling and find a way to respond to this dimension of Second Life's use while holding fast to a largely individualistic picture of its users. A perhaps not surprising effect of this attempt to serve individual choice was the rise of commodification in Second Life. Even if only a small subset of Second Life users are creators of content in any sense, the exercising of individual (consumer) choice amid this array of possibilities was consistent enough with the ideals that underwrite Linden Lab to proceed apace. In this way was *Homo ludens* reconciled with *Homo economicus*.

But to conclude from this that what games and game design have to teach institutions is only how to make markets, at least in the narrowly economic sense, would be a mistake. For both Second Life and itself, Linden Lab's efforts were marked by an awareness that people are motivated by ideals beyond narrow self-interest—the notion of enlightened self-interest lies behind all these efforts, as it did for Stewart Brand's New Communalists. Second Life's "players" are seen as individuals, surely, but also as motivated by interests that may not be quantifiable.

Similarly, it would also be a mistake to infer from Linden Lab's success to this point a kind of "proof" of the surety of their ideals and approach going forward. Nothing about the impressive growth of Second Life during my time there and subsequently should lead us to assume that its continuation has gone, for the Lindens, from a hope to a foregone conclusion. The ideas of Charles Darwin have continually been vulnerable to a misreading that is instructive here; that is, the misguided attempt to impute directionality or normative value to the processes that natural selection identifies (as Menand notes, Darwin regretted even the suggestion of intention that "selection" conveyed; 2001: 122). In my time around Linden Lab I felt it was always a hair's breadth away from flying apart at the seams, and it still may. This is a vital point to keep in mind as we gauge the prospects for ludic bureaucracies.

Another way to put this is that understanding Linden Lab and perhaps similar architects of digital society involves seeing them not only against both the immediate past of the New Communalists, and the larger past of modern bureaucracies, but against the even broader, anthropological interest in how social institutions go about the work of governing, including how they establish their legitimacy over the long term. Political legitimacy remains a core issue for institutions like

Linden Lab, which shape technologized domains like Second Life, precisely because the basis for the legitimacy of their decisions does not fall neatly into familiar categories, such as nationalism, charisma, or even democracy. The imperfect alliance of the bureaucratic state (ordered, ordering) and the nation (meaningful, familial) is not available to Linden Lab, at least currently, precisely because it is built, like a game, on the legitimacy of disorder (as well as, unlike a nation, largely insulated against claims about common history, language, territory, or ethnicity).

To help us think further about political legitimacy, institutions, and digital society, we can turn to work in anthropology on the relationship between political institutions and ritual. For one thing, rituals at first glance seem quite similar to games—they are socially legitimate arenas for the playing out of multiple processes, and they certainly may have unexpected outcomes. Any distinction among them would have to be a relative one and be judged by its usefulness for the questions we wish to ask, but I would in that spirit suggest that while rituals may accidentally result in contingent outcomes, they are for the most part supposed to bring about reliably consistent outcomes. Rituals are sponsored events, and as such reflect the interests of their sponsors, who seek to accomplish something culturally that, yes, may be dangerous or difficult, but which they undertake with at least a guess that they can reliably bring it off. In this way, like bureaucracy, rituals depend on the promise of order, even if in practice their execution opens up contingencies. One example would be the ceremonies for the transfer of names among the Tsimshian of the northwest Pacific coast. The transfer of a ritual name from one individual to another is a fraught and delicate social moment, and things can go wrong (Roth 2002).

But this use of ritual is not confined to nonbureaucratic contexts, to exotic locales still imagined as the province of sociocultural anthropology. For bureaucratic states, ritual can be similarly challenging to pull off successfully, but the stakes can make it worthwhile to try. Susan Gal (1991) documented the attempt by the Hungarian government to prop up its own political legitimacy by bringing the body of Béla Bartók back to the state in the late 1980s. Although Bartók had been buried in New York according to his expressed wishes, the Hungarian government prevailed on his two surviving sons to allow his disinterment, and his body was brought back to Hungary via a pilgrimage through Europe, complete with Bartók music festivals all along the route. The government hoped that by bringing Bartók back, its efforts to maintain a centralized, socialist government would be supported. It would help its own cause by associating itself with a favored son of Hungary, whose elevation of local folk music to the world stage testified to his support of sustaining a local and non-European identity. But the effort backfired dramatically. As Gal charts, Bartók as a symbol could not be controlled, no matter how carefully the government sought to orchestrate its message about him. His physical return to the country prompted, to the government's surprise, *increased* scrutiny of a number of governmental policies, precisely because the multiple meanings and associations that surrounded him were too many for the government to contain in the moment of his remains' immediate presence. He was too polysemic a figure.

A similar question needs to be asked of institutions that are seeking to make room for legitimate indeterminacy. If games provide the primary techniques by which open-endedness can be designed into a "system," can their indeterminacy (which extends to an indeterminacy of meaning) be contained? To what extent does continuing control over the *conditions* of "game play" raise questions of fairness and, ultimately, legitimacy for those participating in the "game"? How can an emerging social division between game players (as makers *within* a system) and game makers (as creators *of* a system) be sustained as new kinds of digital institutions increase the scope of their system-making to include much of our daily activities?

Virtual worlds represent a departure from the bureaucracy of high modernity through their potential to generate meaning and new forms of belonging, and these in ways that at times outstrip the intentions of their creators. This heralds the rise of an unfamiliar ethical relationship between organizations and their projects, one that recognizes, resituates, and seeks to cultivate emergent social phenomena and confounds the well-entrenched modernist aspirations of total control.

What should command the attention of anthropology and the social sciences as a whole is the way in which it is now possible to build, with the help of game design and other techniques, complex spaces designed to be spaces of possibility but without the conventional boundaries that mark games. This generates a remarkable opportunity for us to explore issues such as creativity, governance, ethics, and many others in environments with (at least for now) a different configuration of control from the one that previously marked much of our bureaucratized experience. Institutions, it seems, may be changing in their ability to govern themselves and others, and the advent of virtual worlds is at the forefront of this transformation.

The reason for this development lies in the multiple modes of governance that virtual worlds must, like the broader social world to which they aspire, incorporate. Virtual worlds strive to encompass the material realities in which situated actors find themselves; they are thus constrained and enabled by such factors as architecture, landscape, and resources. The power of architecture online extends to include the governing effects of network protocols, software procedures, interface design, and others. Yet we know that these architectures themselves are subject to exploitation and improvisation in practice. What are the limits of agency as regards not only social convention but also the ubiquitous architectures of technology? What about the role of social convention as a form of governance, and how do virtual worlds become a site for the clash of prior conventions and the generation of new ones? Finally, how do the governing pressures of the market appear within virtual worlds, and how does this constitute a "steering mechanism" as well (to use Habermas's phrase)? Virtual worlds encompass the gamut of these issues, making them ideal cases from which to explore the changing nature of digital governance. I write this book hoping that it will offer a reliable guide to forging an approach for our inquiries into digital society that can encompass both its potential for generating new social forms and its prospects for institutional reproduction; in short, how governance online is a process.

Governance, it is always important to remind ourselves, is not reducible to control. By taking a processual approach to governance, I treat its emergence in and around Linden Lab as a continual and open-ended project, one that encompasses both intentional projects by institutions, groups, and individuals and the unintended consequences that inevitably unfold over time. The contingency inherent in the emergence of new social practices and expectations looms over all aspirations to control, and governance in all its forms is best seen as the outcome of a dance between efforts to control and the various and generative sources of contingency, including improvisation, evasion, and innovation.

What may we call the approach to control through contrived indeterminacy that seems to characterize the descendants of Turner's New Communalists? While inheriting from them a faith in technology, a rejection of top-down control, an imagining of people as individual performers, and a faith in the legitimacy of emergent effects, the descendants have added the aspiration to architect entire, open-ended systems and to incorporate game design into their practice (as did Ken Kesey). In a sense, "technoliberalism" captures some of the main features of this new approach, although the term may not sufficiently emphasize the influence of game design practice. In its favor is the way in which it signals how the legitimacy that emergent effects are granted has its own long history, most often connected to the ideas of Adam Smith and the famous (or infamous) invisible hand. But technoliberalism is not simply neoliberalism in another guise; there are core differences. While Adam Smith conceived of a market that was in a way a natural and ineradicable part of the landscape (based on the human propensity "to truck, barter, and exchange"), and neoliberal thought continues to see the market in this way, technoliberalism holds up the idea that such complex systems can be contrived, in their entirety. The liberal component is the imagined freedom of individuals to perform as such within designed systems, generating collective effects that are thereby legitimate.

It is easy, it seems, to contemplate the current human encounter with digital technologies and conceive, erroneously, of some kind of break from our past—that this technology by itself engenders new ways of thinking and being, disconnected from what has come before.

It is equally important to avoid the social determinist view that nothing is really changed by technology, that everything is old wine in new bottles. We are left as, to a certain degree, particularists, wed to the specific and contingent chain of events that happens, in true Darwinian fashion, to have left us in the current moment. But to see the emergence of the institutions acting as digital architects today is not to marvel only at their peculiarity (although I suspect that many readers are doing just that, and rightly so), but also to see them as raising important ethical questions about how governance is changing, right now.

I introduced ritual into the conversation in this final chapter because its study teaches us how authority has, in many times and places, reproduced itself, largely successfully, amid always changing circumstances. When the anthropologist Marshall Sahlins (1985) considered the apotheosis of Captain Cook, he was able to see how a constellation of events, including some pure accidents (such as the ill-fated return to Hawai'i by Cook for urgent repairs), met a long-existing cultural logic of how power worked for the institutions there (the priesthood and the chieftaincy), leading to a dramatic murder comprehensible as sensible yet not by any means inevitable. For technoliberal institutions, struggling to adjust to postbureaucracy, a similar precariousness may obtain. My sense that Second Life was always on the verge of flying apart at the seams appears as a strong contrast only with the bureaucratic era on the heels of which it has arrived. But although Linden Lab's aim and techniques may be strikingly new, against the larger backdrop of rituals and games across human history, the dilemma of architecting contingency while maintaining authority appears quite long-standing.

APPENDIX A
THE TAO OF LINDEN

On Linden Lab's Web site (http://lindenlab.com/about/tao) there is a statement of the company's approach to work (its mission and culture). This was cited by Lindens as a pretty good approximation of how they did things (meaning that it is at least a good approximation of how they thought they did things). It is reprinted here for reference.

Vision and Mission

"It's our mission to connect us all to an online world that advances the human condition."

Or in other words, we are working to create an online world having the exceptional property that it advances the capabilities of the many people that use it, and by doing so affects and transforms them in a positive way. Read "The Mission of Linden Lab" blog post for more info.

This version of a publicly available document on the Web (http://lindenlab.com/about/tao) was retrieved on March 25, 2008.

Company Principles

Work Together!

The problems we face in creating Second Life are usually larger than one person can solve, and solving them together is one of the great strengths we have as a company. We will succeed only if we collaborate with each other extensively and well. This means helping others reach their goals, asking for help and input often, and being easy to work with. Create teams as necessary to solve specific problems, and support your teammates. Remember that being open and honest is essential but is only the threshold requirement—great collaborative work requires intuitive compassion and support.

Your Choice Is Your Responsibility

There's a dual meaning here.

Most companies tell you what to do. Then they make you accountable to the person who told you what to do, not to yourself. We don't think this gets the best long-term results with a truly ambitious project like Second Life. At Linden Lab, you are expected to choose your own work; you have to decide how you can best move the company forward. This isn't always easy, but it can be very rewarding for you and it is a huge win for the company. This doesn't mean that you can't ask someone else what to do—it means that you are responsible for choosing who to listen to! You are responsible for listening well and broadly enough to choose wisely.

And once you have chosen, you are responsible for executing well to make your choices work. You must understand that other people now rely on you for single-minded execution, and it is time to shut out the noise and work without distraction. Sometimes you will fail, and in those cases it is very important to fail fast and fail publicly—that is how we learn and iterate and ultimately win.

Be Transparent and Open

There are many ways to emphasize responsibility, accountability, communication, and trust. We believe that the one key principle that best supports all of these values is transparency. As much as possible, tell everyone what you are doing, all the time. This transparency makes us responsible to our peers, makes us accountable to our own statements, and replaces the need for management with individual responsibility. Over time, it creates and reinforces trust. Be willing to share ideas before you feel they are "baked." Report on your own progress frequently and to everyone.

Make Weekly Progress

We believe that every person should make specific, visible individual contributions that moves [sic] the company forward every week. Projects must be broken down into measurable tasks so that making weekly progress is possible. This is a principle that almost no one believes is true when they first hear it, yet everyone who keeps to this principle over the course of several months is stunned by the amount of progress made during that time. Set weekly goals and report progress to everyone. Regardless how big what you are working on may be, you can always break it down this way. Give it a try.

No Politics!

Never act to advance your own interests or someone else's interests at the expense of the interests of the company. This is the one principle, outside of violations of law, for which violation will likely result in immediate termination.

Might Makes Right

Just kidding—wanted to make sure you're still paying attention. Lots of things could be said here: Have a sense of humor. Have a sense of humility. Have fun. Call out inconsistency in principles when you see it. Don't let a staid form and function become routine and boilerplate. Which leads to our last principle . . .

Do It with Style

It's not enough that we are changing the world. It's not enough that Second Life is incredibly complex and our vision is vast and shifting.

We're not just going to succeed, we're going to do it with style. As with life, the journey matters as much as the destination. That means a lot of different things, and a lot of what it means can't be captured in words alone. Find out by talking to your colleagues, by living the principles above, and by exploring Second Life.

APPENDIX B

THE MISSION OF LINDEN LAB

The statement below was posted by Philip Rosedale (under his Second Life name Philip Linden) to the official Second Life blog (http://blog.secondlife.com) on Monday, November 6, 2006. It had prompted 196 comments in response as of March 1, 2008. The main post is reprinted here for reference.

The Mission of Linden Lab

Monday, November 6, 2006, at 8:57 AM PST by: Philip Linden
Given the recent tremendous growth of Second Life, I thought it might be of benefit to describe, as best I can, the mission of Linden Lab. Few Second Life residents today will remember the early days of the Second Life environment and community or know that Linden Lab is a seven-year-old company with a rich and interesting history. While such rapid growth is, in the words of investors, a "high-quality problem," it is a problem nonetheless. New residents entering Second

This version of a publicly available document on the Web (http://blog.secondlife.com/ 2006/11/06/the-mission-of-linden-lab/) was retrieved on March 25, 2008.

Life are choosing to commit their time, aspirations, creativity, and dreams to the creation of a shared virtual world. And very unlike the physical world, this virtual world is a place which, at least for the present, has an architecture and business model controlled by a small private company. The power that Linden Lab has to influence the fabric of Second Life is very great, and so I feel we have the responsibility to communicate, as clearly as possible, which way we are headed. Ultimately, I believe that the clearest possible way in which we do this is in our actions, not our words. But I also think that an attempt to provide a statement of intention which can serve as a guidepost by which to measure our efforts is both useful and ultimately part of the value that I, as founder and CEO, should be delivering in my job. Moreover, if I can communicate a clear vision, then perhaps you, as readers, residents, or employees (and in some cases all of the above) will more easily forgive us when we make the mistakes that in our best efforts we will still sometimes make in following this mission.

It is certainly the goal of Linden Lab to operate profitably, and by doing so create returns for the shareholder-owners of the company. The financial history of Linden Lab is the same as that of many other companies: A set of initial investors purchased portions of the company with the expectation that future financial returns would justify the capital they committed. As managers of the company, we are therefore expected to create attractive returns on those investments, or risk being replaced by others who will. But within the broad confines of expected return on investment, there are many different types of investors. Probably the biggest difference is in time horizon: over what period does the investor plan to own their portion of the company? This time horizon can make a big difference in the sort of pressures that owners put on the managers of the company, and therefore a big difference in the way managers make decisions. My own perspective is that many companies today have investors with too short a time horizon, and that technology companies with big projects are particularly liable to this risk, since they may be working on projects that take many years or even decades to fully return value to investors. Within Linden Lab we have a mix of investors with an unusually long time horizon. Looking back I would say we were at first simply very lucky to have such investors (Mitch Kapor being the best and first example), since I knew very little about how to raise investment to finance a company. With learning and the sound counsel of those first investors, we later were able to be more intentional in finding the sort of investors that we believed would have a long time horizon. There are also some investors who have specific principles that they are willing to stick to independent of the impact that these principles may have on the value of their investments. Examples of such principles would include Pierre Omidyar's (one of Linden Lab's owners) desire to invest through his foundation in companies that use technology to improve society, or Warren Buffet's (not a Linden Lab investor) stated intention to not sell companies once he has acquired them even if they are underperforming expectations. These kinds of investors pursue companies that they believe share their principles. Linden Lab is fortunate to have a number of such strongly principled investors, with their intentions loosely grouped around the above-mentioned idea of using technology to advance people. Moreover, I believe that the principles of the investors in Linden Lab are very well aligned with creating great financial returns.

The investor owners of Linden Lab therefore have a mission which is the product of both a longer than average investment timeline, and a set of principles that are shared by a substantial number of the investors. Linden Lab is a company that has required a considerable investment of capital (about $20M will likely have been spent between inception and profitability), and like many other companies of a similar nature is therefore majority-owned by its investors. In my opinion this is a great thing, because we get as a result a diverse set of highly engaged owners with a fairly well shared sense of what they want the company to become. Though I would certainly describe my own vision, management style, and principles as being very well aligned with this diverse set of owners, I think that the company is more likely to succeed and profit long term with such a team rather than a single person in a position of complete control, however smart that one person may be. This basic belief is echoed by the very structure of Second Life—a world created and controlled by many, not few.

Summarizing the exact mission of Linden Lab cannot, given this broad set of owners, ever be done with perfect accuracy—not all of us will agree on the same set of words. But here I believe that our balance of uncertainty and agreement is close to ideal—we have not chosen an uninteresting goal that fails to attract great people and returns, nor have we set our sights so broadly that we will wander and be unlikely to succeed. Given this prelude, my best definition of our mission is that we are working to create an online world having the exceptional property that it advances the capabilities of the many people that use it, and by doing so affects and transforms them in a positive way. More specifically, since there are so many possible definitions of "online world," we are trying to create a close reproduction of the actual physical world we live in—one that will be easily comprehensible and useful to us because it will so closely resemble ours. The ability to simulate our world on computers means that we can make it different in ways that empower us, allowing us to do things that in the physical world we can imagine but are incapable of. Largest among the new capabilities we seek to create through this simulation are: improvements to our ability to communicate quickly and accurately with each other, and the ability to rapidly express our thoughts or intentions as shared artifacts within this new world. This mission is both a great business and a great cause. If we empower people by our efforts, we can expect a fraction of the value of those improvements in return for having built the infrastructure to enable them. Improvement to the capabilities, intelligence, or well-being of a broad group of people has great value. Indeed, I would argue that the greatest technology-driven business success stories have been those like the personal computer or the telephone, in which technology has directly and broadly improved the capabilities of individuals. Second Life and Linden Lab are on their way to becoming one of those stories.

Beyond the details of financial performance, we will have been successful in this mission if we, in the smallest amount of time and capital, make Second Life work as well as possible, given the limits of the underlying computer technology, and reach the largest number of people. You should expect to see the great majority of our efforts directed toward a balance of those two goals. Thus far, I think we have done well. We have certainly made our share of mistakes, but we have managed with a small team to create a very complex software system, scale it under heavy growth, and support the emerging community. As our market space matures and competitors create offerings that are similar to Second Life, I think we will see further validation of the quality of our work.

As a final thought, this mission also suggests things that we will not do. For example, we will not move in a direction that will restrict Second Life as to the number of people it can conceivably reach. This means that we will struggle to have Second Life work in any country, be available to anyone wanting to use it, and work well on a wide range of computing devices. As another example, we will not restrict Second Life by adding constraints which might make it more compelling to a specific subset of people but have the effect of reducing the broadest capabilities it offers to everyone for communication and expression. Both Linden Lab and the community of Second Life residents will likely be tempted with short-term opportunities that are compelling but inconsistent with this longer term mission. I hope that we have built the right company and chosen the right investors to continue to wisely avoid those mistakes. I believe that we have. I thank those who have already joined us in this mission, and invite the rest to join us in the project of a lifetime.

NOTES

Introduction: A Developer's-Eye View

1. They have also been called, variously, massively multiplayer online role-playing games (MMORPGs, or simply MMOGs), massively multiplayer online [worlds] (MMOs), and synthetic worlds (Castronova 2005), but virtual worlds currently enjoys precedence, despite the misleading suggestion that "virtual" makes: that there is a clear separation of it from the "real."

2. This is the number of unique accounts that have logged into Second Life in the past fourteen days as of February 23, 2008. Linden Lab provides a number of regularly updated demographic statistics here: http://secondlife .com/whatis/economy_stats.php. Until mid-2007 Linden Lab's primary statistic for representing its population was "residents," which referred to all accounts that had ever been created (most of them free accounts), a number that surpassed eight million at that time. Since then, Linden Lab has instead provided numbers of users sorted by time of last login (seven, fourteen, thirty, and sixty days) as its primary statistic. It is still difficult to tease out to what degree even these numbers are skewed by the number of new accounts that will never be used again. Also, I chose not to use Linden Lab's term, residents, for Second Life users. While it certainly fits with their marketing efforts, I see no compelling reason for it to stand as an analytic for this or any other virtual world.

3. All Lindens were informed via company e-mail about my research project and given the choice not to participate, which they could invoke at any time. I use pseudonyms or otherwise avoid identifying Lindens who appear in what follows, in quotations or descriptions. At times, I make exceptions for my interviews with Philip Rosedale and other director-level Lindens, who are public figures that represent the company. I also at times refer to public statements that Lindens made elsewhere, such as on Web logs.

4. Linden Lab moved to a new office in April 2005, from an office on Second Street to one near the bluff below Coit Tower. I allude to this move at several points in the chapters that follow. Also, it bears mentioning that the small number of Linden employees makes delving into individual histories next to impossible without revealing enough identifying details to betray actual identities. I focus on the Lindens' work lives to a great extent but even there must avoid giving extensive specifics at times—many of the Lindens continue to work there, and lengthy thick description runs the risk of identification.

5. I also looked for new ways to take advantage of digital media, and in mid-2005 Wagner James Au (a journalist who has covered Second Life for a number of years, at first under a contract relationship with Linden Lab) and I began a Linden Lab History Wiki, to which we invited employees of Linden Lab to add their recollections about Linden Lab's past on a timeline.

6. The island was later named the "Heterocera Atoll" (see http://secondlife .wikia.com/wiki/Heterocera_Atoll, accessed 21 February 2008). This usage suggests that the inspiration for the shape of the landmass may not have been the collapsed volcano of Santorini but rather the circular rings of coral that make up some islands in the South Pacific.

7. It is worth noting that the graphical, avatar-mediated virtual worlds currently prominent owe a great deal of their design to the original text-based virtual worlds, begun in the mid-1970s (see Bartle 2003).

8. Users in Second Life have a special page of their profile dedicated to information about their lives beyond Second Life itself—this tab is labeled "First Life."

9. For an early treatment of similar issues for a text-based virtual world, see Pargman (2000).

10. The picture of bureaucracy here derives from Max Weber (1946), who proposed that bureaucratic authority, in contrast to charismatic and traditional authority, achieves its legitimacy through the necessity of following rules for the sake of following rules. (One recalls the phrase used by the researchers of Stanley Milgram's experiments: "The experiment *must* continue.")

11. For example, new media scholars have sought to develop an approach to games that connects them to critical theory (Bogost 2006; Galloway 2006).

12. See, for example, Burke 2002, 2004; Castronova 2005; Consalvo 2007; Steinkuehler 2006; Taylor and Kolko 2003; and Taylor 2006.

13. On post-bureaucratic organizations and their relationship to ever-changing technology, see Kellogg, Orlikowski, and Yates (2006), and Orlikowski (1996).

Chapter 1. The Product: Second Life, Capital, and the Possibility of Failure in a Virtual World

1. Instant messaging (IM) is also built into Second Life, so users can send private messages to individuals wherever in Second Life they may be.

2. Learning generates competencies; there are other forms of cultural capital—credentials and artifacts—that are generated by other kinds of exchange.

3. See Crump (1981: 8), Simmel (1978: 153), Cohen (1998: 11–12), Leyshon and Thrift (1997), among others.

4. http://news.com.com/Wells+Fargo+launches+game+inside+Second+Life/2100-1043_3-5868030.html.

5. Reciprocity as the basis for the establishment of social relations that could be drawn on to acquire status is classically represented in the "big man" system at one time prevalent in Melanesia. See Sahlins (1963).

6. One account of the event can be found at http://secondlife.blogs.com/nwn/2005/07/day_of_the_doct.html.

7. See http://secondlife.blogs.com/nwn/2005/10/laying_down_the.html.

Chapter 2. Tools of the Gods

1. William Gibson is a perhaps better-known author who wrote about virtual environments in novels such as *Neuromancer* (1984), and his work predates Stephenson's; nonetheless, around Linden Lab Stephenson was cited far more frequently as having provided the model for what Linden Lab was making.

2. In this respect, Tom Boellstorff's identification of the neoliberal underpinnings of Second Life is on target (2008: 209), but it is important to note how the ideas of Brand and others that found their way into Linden Lab did not restrict the arena of the invisible hand to the market alone. The economy of Second Life is indeed "creationist capitalism" of a sort, but the implications

of this faith in aggregated individual performance amid a complex system reach beyond commodities and the market for Brand, following Wiener and Bateson, as Turner (2006) shows.

3. For the developers, there was a constant struggle on the part of Cory Ondrejka and their project managers both to ensure that sufficient developer time was devoted to fixing bugs (generally an undesirable task) and that new developers were not the ones saddled disproportionately with this kind of work.

4. Another interesting development which came after I completed my research was the opening up of portions of Linden Lab's Jira to users (and anyone—it is available on the Web at https://jira.secondlife.com) for their comments and votes. Discussion of this will have to await further research.

5. This is also an abbreviation for "peer-to-peer," as in P2P networks—there are possible connections to be drawn between these uses, but they lie outside the scope of this chapter.

6. Another option was for another user to "Offer a Teleport" to their current location, which would allow P2P, provided there was a contact at the location to ask.

Chapter 3. Knowing the Gamer from the Game

1. For a more detailed argument on why games should not be viewed simply as play, see Malaby 2007a.

2. Process in this recursive sense is a concept that may be best understood as situated within the history of American thought, specifically pragmatism and semiotics (Peirce 1998; see also Menand 2001), but one finds it in many schools of thought, although often under different names. The concept can also be found, with some variations in meaning, in legal realism and the anthropology of law (Moore 1978), Marx (1978), phenomenology (Jackson 1989), ritual studies (Turner 1969; "ritual as process"), performance theory (Bauman 1977; the "emergent quality of performance"), practice theory (Ortner 1984), and science and technology studies (STS; Pickering 1995; the "mangle of practice"). We are also seeing important gestures in this direction from game scholarship (Galloway 2006, Taylor 2006, Steinkuehler 2006).

3. A significant history remains to be written about the early period of computer games, when an accommodation in practice had to be reached between highly rationalized, Boolean code and the demands to provide contingency in games.

4. For more on game constraints, see Malaby 2006b.

5. This aspiration to something between top-down control and laissez-faire faith in emergence also appears under other names. See, for example, Richard Thaler and Cass Sunstein's (2008) argument in favor of "libertarian paternalism."

6. This randomness need not be "true" randomness; it need be only practically random; that is, indistinguishable from true randomness from the point of view of the participant (allowing for any technological or other aids available to him or her to identify patterns and thereby recognize it as otherwise).

7. For an extended discussion of the potential of gaming events to transform local meanings, see Malaby 1999.

8. See also Julian Dibbell's (1998) landmark account of LambdaMOO, the text-based virtual world, in which his own Herculean effort to build a garden of forking paths based on the *I Ching* figures prominently.

9. See also the game of Dealer discussed by Michael Hiltzik in his book on Xerox PARC (2000: 145–150). There, too, the appeal to a gamelike system of redistributing authority masked the ways in which certain established power structures went unchallenged (149).

10. A summary of the Elo rating system and links to further resources were found at http://en.wikipedia.org/wiki/Elo_rating_system on March 27, 2007.

11. My thanks to Bonnie Nardi for helping me develop this characterization of play as a disposition.

12. This is clear in various respects in the work of, for example, Pierre Bourdieu (1977), Michel de Certeau (1984), Anthony Giddens (1984), and Marshall Sahlins (1985).

13. As a postscript to these efforts to use voting to generate priorities out of Jira, Linden Lab opened up voting for some Jira tasks after I completed my research. At http://jira.secondlife.com Second Life users can sort, read through descriptions about, and vote on any of a set (not complete) of Jira tasks for Linden Lab to complete. In this way, again, Linden Lab sought to provide access to tools for individuals whose collective action would issue forth in collective wisdom, while maintaining its position as the maker of the larger game.

Chapter 4. The Birth of the Cool

1. As a result, I found the "collaborative creativity" phrase somewhat out of keeping with the individualist emphasis I saw elsewhere around Linden Lab. On gently inquiring further, I learned how the trope may have appeared. One Linden from the marketing department pointed to the period when Linden Lab

was trying (ultimately successfully) to court Pierre Omidyar (founder of eBay) as an investor. That was when, the Linden told me, Linden Lab began to highlight collaboration in its marketing and other materials.[0]

2. The original, in translation, is, "Let a hundred flowers bloom; let a hundred schools of thought contend" (see http://en.wikipedia.org/wiki/Hundred _Flowers_Campaign, accessed March 12, 2008). There are multiple ironies in the Linden Lab invocation of that phrase, given its original use, but I do not discuss them here.

BIBLIOGRAPHY

Aneesh, A. 2006. *Virtual Migration: The Programming of Globalization.* Durham, N.C.: Duke University Press.

Austin, J. L. 1975. *How to Do Things with Words.* 2d ed. Cambridge, Mass.: Harvard.

Barbrook, Richard, and Andy Cameron. 2001. "Californian Ideology." In *Crypto Anarchy, Cyberstates, and Pirate Utopias,* edited by Peter Ludlow, 363–387. Cambridge, Mass.: MIT Press.

Bartle, Richard. 2003. *Designing Virtual Worlds.* Indianapolis: New Riders.

Bauman, Richard. 1977. "Verbal Art as Performance." In *Verbal Art as Performance,* edited by Richard Bauman, 3–58. Prospect Heights: Waveland Press.

Bergson, Henri. 1911. *Creative Evolution.* New York: Henry Holt.

Boellstorff, Tom. 2008. *Coming of Age in Second Life: An Anthropologist Explores the Virtual Human.* Princeton, N.J.: Princeton University Press.

Bogost, Ian. 2006. *Unit Operations: An Approach to Videogame Criticism.* Cambridge, Mass.: MIT Press.

Bourdain, Anthony. 2007. *Kitchen Confidential: Adventures in the Culinary Underbelly.* Updated ed. New York: Harper Perennial.

Bourdieu, Pierre. 1977. *Outline of a Theory of Practice.* Translated by Richard Nice. Cambridge: Cambridge University Press.

——. 1986. "The Forms of Capital." In *Handbook of Theory and Research in the Sociology of Education,* edited by J. Richardson, 241–258. Westport, Conn.: Greenwood.

——. 1999. *Language and Symbolic Power.* Translated by Gino Raymond and Matthew Adamson. Cambridge, Mass.: Harvard University Press.

Braman, Sandra. 2007. *Change of State: Information, Policy, and Power.* Cambridge, Mass.: MIT Press.

Brand, Stewart, ed. 1969. *Whole Earth Catalog: Access to Tools.* Menlo Park, Calif.: Portola Institute.

Burke, Timothy. 1996. *Lifebuoy Men, Lux Women: Commodification, Consumption, and Cleanliness in Modern Zimbabwe.* Durham, N.C.: Duke University Press.

——. 2002. "Rubicite Breastplate Priced to Move, Cheap: How Virtual Economies Become Real Simulations." Retrieved July 31, 2006, from www.swarthmore.edu/SocSci/tburke1/Rubicite%20Breastplate.pdf.

——. 2004. "Play of State: Sovereignty and Governance in MMOGs." Retrieved April 22, 2008, from http://weblogs.swarthmore.edu/burke/?page_id=32.

Caillois, Roger. 1961. *Man, Play, and Games.* Translated by Meyer Barash. New York: Free Press.

Call, Eric. 2005. "Making Machinima in Second Life." Retrieved March 12, 2008, from http://s3.amazonaws.com/static-secondlife-com/_files/making_machinima.pdf.

Calleja, Gordon. 2007. "Digital Game Involvement: A Conceptual Model." *Games and Culture* 2 (3): 236–260.

Carr, David F. 2007. "How Google Works." *Baseline Magazine* (online). Retrieved February 28, 2008, from www.baselinemag.com/c/a/Projects-Networks-and-Storage/How-Google-Works-%5B1%5D/.

Cassell, Justine, and Henry Jenkins, eds. 1998. *From Barbie to Mortal Kombat: Gender and Computer Games.* Cambridge, Mass.: MIT Press.

Castronova, Edward. 2005. *Synthetic Worlds: The Business and Culture of Online Games.* Chicago: University of Chicago Press.

Certeau, Michel de. 1984. *The Practice of Everyday Life.* Translated by Steven Rendall. Berkeley: University of California Press.

Coca-Cola, Inc. 2007. "Coca-Cola Launches Competition to Design Online 'Virtual Thirst' Coke Machine. Press Release, April 16, 2007. Retrieved April 27, 2008, from www.virtualthirst.com/pressrelease.html.

Cohen, B. J. 1998. *The Geography of Money.* Ithaca, N.Y.: Cornell University Press.

Coleman, Gabriella. 2004. "The Political Agnosticism of Free and Open Source Software and the Inadvertent Politics of Contrast." *Anthropological Quarterly* 77 (3): 507–519.

Combs, Nate. 2006. "Penguins and Puffins." Retrieved March 1, 2008, from http://terranova.blogs.com/terra_nova/2006/12/the_mmo_univers.html.

Consalvo, Mia. 2007. *Cheating: Gaining Advantage in Video Games*. Cambridge, Mass.: MIT Press.

Crawford, Susan. 2005. "Shortness of Vision: Regulatory Ambition in the Digital Age." Retrieved January 5, 2006, from the SSRN Web site: http://papers.ssrn.com/sol3/papers.cfm?abstract_id=681409.

Crump, T. 1981. *The Phenomenon of Money*. Boston: Routledge and Kegan Paul.

Csikszentmihalyi, M. 1990. *Flow: The Psychology of Optimal Experience*. New York: Harper and Row.

Dibbell, Julian. 1998. *My Tiny Life: Crime and Passion in a Virtual World, Being a True Account of the Case of the Infamous Mr. Bungle, and of the Author's Journey, in Consequence Thereof, to the Heart of the Half-Real World Called LambdaMOO*. New York: Henry Holt.

——. 2006. *Play Money: Or, How I Quit My Day Job and Made Millions Trading Virtual Loot*. New York: Basic Books.

——. 2008. "Mutilated Furries, Flying Phalluses: Put the Blame on Griefers, the Sociopaths of the Virtual World." *Wired*. Retrieved March 1, 2008 from www.wired.com/gaming/virtualworlds/magazine/16–02/mf_goons.

Doctorow, Cory. 2005. *Someone Comes to Town, Someone Leaves Town*. New York: Tor Books.

Dominguez, V. 1990. "Representing Value and the Value of Representation: A Different Look at Money." *Cultural Anthropology* 5 (1): 16–44.

Dornfeld, Robert. 1998. *Producing Public Television, Producing Public Culture*. Princeton, N.J.: Princeton University Press.

Downey, Gary Lee. 1998. *The Machine in Me: An Anthropologist Sits among Software Engineers*. New York: Routledge.

Drucker, Peter F. 1954. *The Practice of Management*. New York: Harper and Row.

Ducheneaut, N., Moore, R. J., and Nickell, E. 2007. "Virtual Third Places: A Case Study of Sociability in Massively Multiplayer Games." *Computer Supported Cooperative Work*, 16 (1–2): 129–166.

Elo, Arpad E. 1978. *The Rating of Chessplayers, Past and Present*. New York: Arco.

Fine, Gary Alan. 1996. *Kitchens: The Culture of Restaurant Work*. Berkeley: University of California Press.

Foucault, Michel. 1977. *Discipline and Punish*. Translated by Alan Sheridan. London: Allen Lane.

Gal, Susan. 1991. "Bartók's Funeral: Representations of Europe in Hungarian Political Rhetoric." *American Ethnologist* 18: 440–458.

Galloway, Alexander. 2006. *Gaming: Essays on Algorithmic Culture*. Minneapolis: University of Minnesota Press.

Gee, J. P. 2003. *What Video Games Have to Teach Us about Learning and Literacy*. New York: Palgrave MacMillan.

Gibson, William. 1984. *Neuromancer*. New York: Ace Books.

Giddens, Anthony. 1984. *The Constitution of Society: Outline of the Theory of Structuration*. Cambridge: Polity.

Goffman, Erving. 1959. *The Presentation of Self in Everyday Life*. Garden City, N.Y.: Doubleday.

Habermas, Jürgen. 1987. *The Theory of Communicative Action*, vol. 2. Translated by Thomas McCarthy. Boston: Beacon Press.

Helmreich, Stefan. 1998. *Silicon Second Nature*. Berkeley: University of California Press.

Herzfeld, Michael. 1993. *The Social Production of Indifference: Exploring the Roots of Western Bureaucracy*. Chicago: University of Chicago Press.

Hiltzik, Michael A. 2000. *Dealers of Lightning: Xerox PARC and the Dawn of the Computer Age*. New York: Collins.

Huizinga, Johan. 1955. *Homo Ludens: A Study of the Play-Element in Culture*. Translated by R. F. C. Hull. Boston: Beacon Press.

Jackson, Michael. 1989. *Paths Toward a Clearing: Radical Empiricism and Ethnographic Inquiry*. Bloomington: Indiana University Press.

Jacobs, Jane. 1961. *The Death and Life of Great American Cities*. New York: Random House.

Karabel, Jerome. 2005. *The Chosen: The Hidden History of Admission and Exclusion at Harvard, Yale, and Princeton*. Boston: Houghton Mifflin.

Kellogg, Katherine, Wanda J. Orlikowski, and Joanne Yates. 2006. "Life in the Trading Zone: Structuring Coordination across Boundaries in Post-Bureaucratic Organizations." *Organization Science* 17 (1): 22–44.

Kelty, Christopher. 2005. "Geeks, Social Imaginaries, and Recursive Publics." *Cultural Anthropology* 20 (2): 185–214.

Kidder, Tracy. 1981. *The Soul of a New Machine*. Boston: Little, Brown.

Kitchin, Rob, and Martin Dodge. 2006. "Software and the Mundane Management of Air Travel." *First Monday*, special issue no. 7, edited by Sandra Braman and Thomas Malaby. http://firstmonday.org/issues/special11_9/intro/index.html.

Lastowka, F. Gregory, and Dan Hunter. 2003. "The Laws of the Virtual Worlds." *California Law Review*. Retrieved January 5, 2006, from the SSRN Web site: http://ssrn.com/abstract=402860.

Lessig, Lawrence. 1999. *Code and Other Laws of Cyberspace*. New York: Basic Books.

Levy, Steven. 1984. *Hackers: Heroes of the Computer Revolution*. New York: Doubleday.

Leyshon, A., and N. Thrift. 1997. *Money/Space: Geographies of Monetary Transformation*. New York: Routledge.

Llewelyn, Gwyneth. 2005. "It's a Country?" Retrieved March 1, 2008, from http://gwynethllewelyn.net/2005/11/27/its-a-country/.

MacIntyre, Alasdair. 1984. *After Virtue*, 2d ed. Notre Dame, Ind.: University of Notre Dame Press.

Malaby, Thomas. 1999. "Fateful Misconceptions: Rethinking Paradigms of Chance among Gamblers in Crete." *Social Analysis* 43 (1): 141–164.

——. 2003a. *Gambling Life: Dealing in Contingency in a Greek City*. Urbana: University of Illinois Press.

——. 2003b. "The Currency of Proof: Euro Competence and the Refiguring of Value in Greece." *Social Analysis* 47 (1): 42–52.

——. 2006a. "Parlaying Value: Forms of Capital in and beyond Virtual Worlds." *Games and Culture* 1 (2): 141–162.

——. 2006b. "Introduction: Control and Contingency Online." *First Monday*, special issue no. 7, edited by Sandra Braman and Thomas Malaby. http://firstmonday.org/issues/special11_9/intro/index.html.

——. 2006c. "Coding Control: Governance and Contingency in the Production of Online Worlds." *First Monday*, special issue no. 7, edited by Sandra Braman and Thomas Malaby. http://firstmonday.org/issues/special11_9/intro/index.html.

——. 2007a. "Beyond Play: A New Approach to Games." *Games and Culture* 2 (2): 95–113.

——. 2007b. "Contriving Constraints: The Gameness of *Second Life* and the Persistence of Scarcity." *Innovations: Technology, Governance, Globalization* 2 (3): 62–67.

Malone, Krista-Lee. 2007. "Dragon Kill Points: The Economics of Power Gamers." Available at the SSRN Web site: http://ssrn.com/abstract=1008035.

Malone, Thomas. 2004. *The Future of Work: How the New Order of Business Will Shape Your Organization, Your Management Style, and Your Life*. Cambridge, Mass.: Harvard Business School Press.

Markoff, John. 2005. *What the Dormouse Said: How the 60s Counterculture Shaped the Personal Computer*. New York: Viking Adult.

Marx, Karl. 1978. "Theses on Feuerbach." In *The Marx-Engels Reader*, edited by Robert C. Tucker, 143–145. New York: W. W. Norton.

Mauss, Marcel. 1967. *The Gift: Forms and Functions of Exchange in Archaic Societies.* Translated by Ian Cunnison. New York: W. W. Norton.

Menand, Louis. 2001. *The Metaphysical Club: A Story of Ideas in America.* New York: Farrar, Straus, and Giroux.

Moore, Sally Falk. 1978. *Law as Process: An Anthropological Approach.* Boston: Routledge and Kegan Paul.

———. 1987. "Explaining the Present: Theoretical Dilemmas in Processual Ethnography." *American Ethnologist* 14 (4): 727–736.

Ondrejka, Cory. 2007. "Collapsing Geography: Second Life, Innovation, and the Future of National Power." *Innovations: Technology, Governance, Globalization* 2 (3): 27–54.

Orlikowski, Wanda J. 1996. "Improvising Organizational Transformation over Time: A Situated Change Perspective." *Information Systems Research* 7 (1): 63–92.

Orr, Julian E. 1996. *Talking about Machines: An Ethnography of a Modern Job.* Ithaca, N.Y.: Cornell University Press.

Ortner, Sherry B. 1984. "Theory in Anthropology since the Sixties." *Comparative Studies in Society and History* 26 (1): 126–166.

Pargman, D. 2000. "Code Begets Community: On Social and Technical Aspects of Managing a Virtual Community." Ph.D. dissertation, Linkoping University. Retrieved June 27, 2008, from http://xml.nada.kth.se/~pargman/thesis/.

Parry, Jonathan P., and Maurice Bloch, eds. 1989. *Money and the Morality of Exchange.* Cambridge: Cambridge University Press.

Paul, Christine. 2006. "Digital Art/Public Art: Governance and Agency in the Networked Commons." *First Monday*, special issue no. 7, edited by Sandra Braman and Thomas Malaby. http://firstmonday.org/issues/special11_9/intro/index.html.

Peirce, Charles S. 1998. *The Essential Peirce: Selected Philosophical Writings, 1893–1913.* Bloomington: Indiana University Press.

Pickering, Andrew. 1995. *The Mangle of Practice: Time, Agency, and Science.* Chicago: University of Chicago Press.

Putnam, Robert D. 2001. *Bowling Alone: The Collapse and Revival of American Community.* New York: Simon and Schuster.

Rabinow, Paul. 1996. *Making PCR: A Study in Biotechnology.* Chicago: University of Chicago Press.

Reid, Chris. 2008. "Machinima: A New Art Form Faces Legal Uncertainty." Retrieved June 25, 2008, from http://iplj.net/blog/2008/01/23/machinima-a-new-art-form-faces-legal-uncertainty/.

Riskin, Jessica. 2003. "The Defecating Duck, or, the Ambiguous Origins of Artificial Life." *Critical Inquiry* 29 (4): 599–633.

Roth, Christopher F. 2002. "Goods, Names, and Selves: Rethinking the Tsim-shian Potlatch." *American Ethnologist* 29 (1): 123–150.

Sahlins, Marshall. 1963. "Poor Man, Rich Man, Big-man, Chief: Political Types in Melanesia and Polynesia." *Comparative Studies in Society and History* 5: 285–303.

——. 1985. *Islands of History*. Chicago: University of Chicago Press.

Simmel, G. 1978. *The Philosophy of Money*. Translated by Tom Bottomore and David Frisby. London: Routledge and Kegan Paul.

Steinkuehler, Constance. 2006. "The Mangle of Play." *Games and Culture* 1 (3): 199–213.

Stephenson, Neal. 1992. *Snow Crash*. New York: Bantam Books.

Stevens, Jr., Phillips. 1980. "Play and Work: A False Dichotomy?" In *Play and Culture*, edited by Helen B. Schwartzman, 316–323. West Point, N.Y.: Leisure Press.

Surowiecki, James. 2004. *The Wisdom of Crowds: Why the Many are Smarter than the Few and How Collective Wisdom Shapes Business, Economies, Societies, and Nations*. New York: Doubleday.

Taylor, T. L. 2006. *Play between Worlds: Exploring Online Game Culture*. Cambridge, Mass.: MIT Press.

Taylor, T. L., and Beth E. Kolko. 2003. "Boundary Spaces: Majestic and the Uncertain Status of Knowledge, Community, and Self in a Digital Age." *Information, Communication, and Society* 6 (4): 497–522.

Thaler, Richard H., and Cass R. Sunstein. 2008. *Nudge: Improving Decisions about Health, Wealth, and Happiness*. New Haven: Yale University Press.

Thomas, Douglas. 2003. *Hacker Culture*. Minneapolis: University of Minnesota Press.

Tilgher, Adriano. 1930. *Homo Faber: Work through the Ages*. Chicago: Henry Regnery.

Turner, Fred. 2006. *From Counterculture to Cyberculture: Stewart Brand, the Whole Earth Network, and the Rise of Digital Utopianism*. Chicago: University of Chicago Press.

Turner, Victor. 1969. *The Ritual Process: Structure and Anti-Structure*. New York: Walter de Gruyter.

Waldrop, M. Mitchell. 2001. *The Dream Machine: J. C. R. Licklider and the Revolution That Made Computing Personal*. New York: Viking Adult.

Weber, Max. 1946. *From Max Weber: Essays in Sociology*, edited by H. H. Gerth and C. Wright Mills. Oxford: Oxford University Press.

Williams, Dmitri. 2006. "Groups and Goblins: The Social and Civil Impact of an Online Game." *Journal of Broadcasting and Electronic Media* 50 (4): 651–670.

INDEX

Page numbers with an *f* indicate figures.